ASYLUM

UNDERSTANDING PUBLIC ATTITUDES

MIRANDA LEWIS

ippr

The **Institute for Public Policy Research** (ippr) is the UK's leading progressive think tank and was established in 1988. Its role is to bridge the political divide between the social democratic and liberal traditions, the intellectual divide between academia and the policy making establishment and the cultural divide between government and civil society. It is first and foremost a research institute, aiming to provide innovative and credible policy solutions. Its work, the questions its research poses and the methods it uses are driven by the belief that the journey to a good society is one that places social justice, democratic participation and economic and environmental sustainability at its core.

For further information you can contact ippr's external affairs department on info@ippr.org, you can view our website at www.ippr.org and you can buy our books from Central Books on 0845 458 9910 or email ippr@centralbooks.com.

CONTENTS

Foreword

by Trevor Phillips OBE, Chair, Commission for Racial Equality

The recent general election showed that vilifying and degrading asylum seekers is popular with some of the public and some sections of the media. The consequences for race equality and particularly for ensuring good race relations between communities are immense.

The language of resentment is not new, and is reminiscent of the attitudes towards Jewish refugees at the turn of the twentieth century or responses to the Windrush generation. We have a moral obligation to those fleeing persecution and this is backed up by a legal obligation as the UK is signatory to the 1951 Refugee Convention, incorporated into UK law in 1993.

But we must go further, and recognise that refugees and other immigrants provide Britain with major economic, social and cultural benefits, not least a huge injection of character into our society.

This work is therefore particularly timely. The report has involved extensive primary research and brings the latest thinking on the subject to our attention. As Chair of the Commission for Racial Equality, I will be actively considering how its recommendations fit our work, and how the report can inform our work. I urge others to do the same.

Acknowledgements

ippr would like to thank Birmingham City Council, the London Borough of Camden, the Commission for Racial Equality, the National Assembly for Wales and Norwich City Council for their generous financial support for this research project, as well as for their intellectual input. The report represents the views of the authors and not necessarily those of our funders.

Thanks to Laura Edwards, Francesca Hopwood Road and Jack Leather who carried out much of the field work, and to Elli Passmore who undertook some of the background research. Heaven Crawley established the project whilst at ippr, undertook the mapping exercises in the regions and review of existing literature, and contributed to earlier drafts. Thanks also to Nick Pearce, Howard Reed, Rachel O'Brien, Danny Sriskandarajah and Sarah Kyambi for their extensive and very helpful comments on early drafts. John Schwartz and Nicolas Thorner (ippr) helped greatly with the publication of this report.

Thanks also to the people in the regions and to others whom we consulted. A list of interviewees is given in Annex 1. Particular thanks to all those who participated in the focus groups.

Some of the recommendations were developed following an expert round-table at ippr's offices in February 2005. A list of the attendees is given in Annex 2 – thanks to all who attended.

About the author

Miranda Lewis is a Senior Research Fellow at ippr. She heads the People and Policy team, which is at the forefront of developing new methods of public involvement in decision-making. The team promotes good practice and develops criteria for evaluating public involvement methods.

Miranda has considerable experience of designing and using a wide variety of qualitative research methodologies to explore attitudes of a wide range of groups to public policy issues. Her experience includes running focus groups, interviews and large scale public involvement events to ensure that the public voice is represented in discussions about policy. She has also carried out qualitative research projects in developing countries.

Acronyms and definitions

ABC1	Upper to lower middle classes
C2DE	Skilled working class to those at the lowest levels of subsistence
CRE	Commission for Racial Equality
BME	Black and minority ethnic
BNP	British National Party
ICAR	Information Centre about Asylum Seekers and Refugees in the UK
IND	Immigration and Nationality Directorate
NASS	National Asylum Support Service
NNREC	Norwich and Norfolk Race Equality Council
PCC	Press Complaints Commission
UKIP	UK Independence Party

List of tables and charts

Tables

Charts

1. Introduction

Immigration is currently dominating the public imagination. British people are increasingly anxious about the scale of immigration into the UK and its impacts on Britain's economy and society. Asylum seekers have become the subject of a concern which is disproportionate to the actual impact of their presence. Concern has sometimes turned into fear and anger. This is deeply worrying not only for those who have the right to protection, but also for race relations more broadly.

The number of people seeking asylum has risen since 1997. Public anxiety has risen over the same period, but this is not a straightforward matter of cause and effect. Concern is often highest in areas where few or no asylum seekers have been dispersed. There is little public understanding about the distinction between asylum seekers and other immigrants, or about the UK's responsibilities to them.

Public concern also mirrors increased numbers of media reports about asylum, and political tensions over immigration. The Government has responded to this anxiety with legislation aimed at reducing the numbers of asylum seekers by speeding up the process, limiting abuse of the system and increasing removals. There have also been substantial changes in the welfare arrangements for asylum seekers with the creation of the National Asylum Support Service (NASS) and the dispersal policy. Yet these measures have done little to reassure the public that asylum seekers do not pose a significant threat.

To some extent fears about immigration are cyclical, surfacing in 'moral panics' every few years. This goes back for centuries. However, Britain is now a more diverse society than ever before. This means that concerns about immigration and asylum link into other widespread concerns about race, diversity and Britain's role in the world. It also means that they pose far more potential damage to community cohesion.

ippr undertook extensive primary research to understand the reasons for increasingly negative public attitudes towards asylum seekers. It identifies policy levers with which to move towards a more informed public debate. It considers a number of key questions:

- To what extent do increasingly negative attitudes towards asylum seekers reflect the actual economic and social impacts?

- Are attitudes towards asylum seekers a new form of racism? To what extent do they have the potential to undermine the fairly good race relations developed over the past 40 years?

- What role do the media and politicians play in framing the asylum debate and in shaping public attitudes towards asylum seekers, immigrants and minority ethnic groups more generally? What else influences people attitudes to asylum?

- Given that the nature of our society has changed and is changing, what needs to happen at the local and national level to influence people's attitudes and improve social cohesion in communities?

Public opinion and asylum: what we already know

Opinion polls show that public opinion about immigration has become markedly less tolerant over the last decade. Common sentiments identified in surveys are that 'there are too many in Britain', that 'they get too much help' and that 'immigration is out of control' (Saggar and Drean, 2001).

In 1995, around two thirds of the population thought the number of immigrants should be reduced, but by 2003 this had jumped to three quarters. All of this increase was among those who thought the number of immigrants should be reduced 'a lot'. Meanwhile, the proportion that thought immigration should stay at the same level or be increased had fallen from just under a third to a fifth (McLaren and Johnson, 2004).

Table 1: Recent opinion poll findings

- In 2000 a MORI poll for the Reader's Digest found that two thirds of respondents felt that there were too many immigrants in Britain; and 80 per cent of respondents agreed that 'asylum seekers come to the UK because they regard Britain as a "soft touch"' (MORI, 2000).

- An ICM poll conducted for the *Guardian* in May 2001 found that 70 per cent of the British public would support a decision to allow more immigration from people who had skills that were in short supply here. The survey also revealed that there were significant variations in attitudes towards asylum seekers from different countries of origin.

- A YouGov survey prepared for the *Sun* newspaper in 2003 identified immigration and asylum seekers as the most important political issue facing the UK (39 per cent felt this) (YouGov, 2003).

- A MORI survey of prejudice undertaken for Stonewall in 2003 found that almost two thirds of people in England (64 per cent) could name at least one minority group towards whom they felt less positive. Around one in three people felt less positive towards refugees and asylum seekers (Stonewall, 2003).

- A YouGov survey for *The Economist* found that the vast majority of respondents (85 per cent) agreed that Britain would need more skilled and/or unskilled workers over the next five years. Despite this, 74 per cent of respondents also agreed with the statement that 'too many immigrants are coming to Britain' and 52 per cent expressed concern that 'too many asylum seekers are let in' (YouGov, 2004a).

MORI surveys of British attitudes show a major increase in those who see immigration as the most important issue facing Britain (Page, 2004). Prior to this around 5 per cent of people identified race relations and immigration as a national issue of concern. Since the late 1990s these issues have soared up the public agenda, and are now in the top three national concerns. Chart 1 shows that in February 2005 race relations and immigration formed the single most important issue in the minds of the British population.

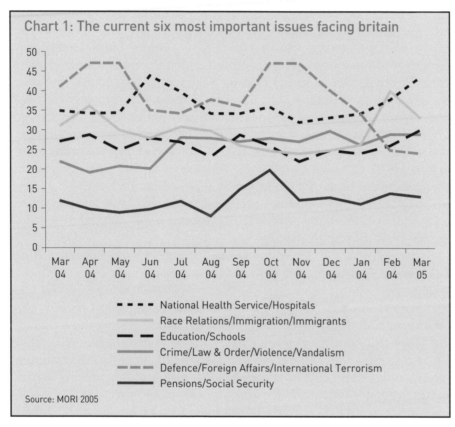

Chart 1: The current six most important issues facing britain

- - - National Health Service/Hospitals
Race Relations/Immigration/Immigrants
- - Education/Schools
Crime/Law & Order/Violence/Vandalism
- - - Defence/Foreign Affairs/International Terrorism
Pensions/Social Security

Source: MORI 2005

Uneasiness about immigration is common across Europe, but British citizens are more hostile than those of other European countries. European Commission research finds that in the UK there is 'often exasperation at the phenomenon of immigration and the scale it has reached' (European Commission, 2003), with particular concern among middle to lower social classes. A recent Eurobarometer survey found that the proportion of British respondents who believe that legal immigrants should have the same rights as nationals is among the lowest in Europe. This is despite relatively widespread recognition that immigrants are needed to fill gaps in the UK labour market (European Commission, 2004).

The case for more research

Despite this wealth of data, policy makers need new evidence. Opinion polls and attitudes surveys tell us what people think about particular issues but they cannot tell us *why* they hold these attitudes.

Few of the opinion polls described in the previous section specifically address the issue of asylum. Most are framed in terms of general immigration issues. Yet findings from polls on race and immigration have also been used to tell a story about asylum. The terms race/immigration and asylum are often used interchangeably, both by the public and people carrying out survey work. Migration Watch UK (an anti-immigration organisation) recently commissioned a survey of attitudes to multi-culturalism and immigration from polling company YouGov (Migration Watch 2005). This asked broad questions about British culture and immigration. None of the questions were concerned with asylum, yet the poll is described on the Migration Watch website as an 'opinion poll on asylum and immigration'.

Opinion polls tend to assume a degree of knowledge about the issues involved. This can pose a problem in relation to asylum and immigration, where there is widespread confusion about the facts; for example, a survey which asks whether the level of immigration into the UK should be increased or reduced assumes that respondents have some knowledge of existing levels of immigration.

Some opinion polls are commissioned specifically to achieve a particular objective. This is reflected in the use of loaded questions. For example, a YouGov poll commissioned by the *Sun* newspaper (YouGov, 2003) asks respondents whether they consider that 'some parts of British cities have become so completely taken over by immigrant communities that they are no longer truly British'. Respondents were also asked to agree or disagree with a statement that 'immigrants often fail to mix properly with the rest of society, and merely congregate together'. The poll was then used to conflate concerns about British society with asylum (*Sun*, 18 August 2003).[1]

Some more detailed research into attitudes towards immigration has been carried out. McLaren and Johnson (2004) examine six hypotheses in an attempt to understand why there has been an increase in negative attitudes towards immigration. Valentine and McDonald (2004) have also carried out research across local areas and different socio-economic and demographic groups in an attempt to better understand attitudes and what shapes them. However these do not look specifically at asylum seekers. ippr wanted to focus upon asylum rather than upon immigration more broadly specifically because of the Government's responsibility for protection to this group.

---

1 The article reads: '[t]he flood of asylum cheats brought by criminal gangs has soured the otherwise tolerant attitudes towards foreigners. Three out of four adults say some city suburbs have become so taken over by immigrant communities that they are "no longer truly British"'.

Methodology

ippr's aim was to explain what lies behind these increasingly negative public attitudes. We carried out qualitative research in different areas with a range of groups from different socio-economic and demographic backgrounds. This allowed us to unpick perceptions of impacts from actual impacts and to compare data both vertically (by area) and horizontally (by different social group). While the research sought to map public opinion against the impacts, it was not designed specifically to track down myths or to challenge every negative perception.

Research took place in Birmingham, Cardiff, Camden, Norwich and Weymouth.[2] These are all very different in terms of their experience of hosting asylum seekers, social and economic contexts, previous history of immigration and ethnic mix. Mapping exercises were undertaken in each of the areas. This included interviews with 36 local stakeholders (Annex 1), research into census data, local press activity and NASS figures. This allowed us to develop a picture of the local context and policies in each area.

ippr held focus groups in each area. This gave us the opportunity to hold in-depth discussions with a large number of participants. In total there were 32 focus groups with a total of 227 participants. Each focus group had between six to eight participants from a similar age, class or ethnic origin. There were equal numbers of women and men in each group, with the exception of the Somali group in Cardiff, where cultural mores meant that was not possible for women to attend the meeting.

Groups were:

- Social classes ABC1 (middle class) aged 25 to 50

- Social classes C2DE (working class) living in social housing aged 25 to 50

- Social classes ABC1 (middle class) aged 51 or over

- Social classes C2DE (working class) living in social housing aged 51 or over

- People from black and minority ethnic (BME) backgrounds (recruited to reflect the largest ethnic groups in each area).[3]

- Young people aged 17 to 19.

Splitting the groups by social class enabled the researchers to analyse the impact of economic concerns on attitudes to asylum seekers. People from BME groups are over-represented in relation to overall population. As the

---

2   Despite similarities with some inner London boroughs, Camden has a unique context and should not be assumed to be a representative London case study. In particular there is considerable socio-economic polarisation.

3   Where possible each group consisted of people from a particular ethnic background or community. This was not possible in either Weymouth or Norwich because of the small numbers of people from BME backgrounds living in those areas.

issue of race relations is increasingly being used as a justification for tough policies on asylum, gaining a thorough understanding of these groups' attitudes was particularly important. The diversity of the minority ethnic communities also allowed us to analyse variations in attitudes between different groups.

Focus groups made up of participants from similar backgrounds had the advantage of making the participants feel comfortable in a more natural setting. They also allowed insight into how groups collectively formed opinions, negotiated their differences and took up positions by framing issues in relation to their own experiences. Structuring the groups in this way allowed us to analyse the relative importance of different factors, including social background, age, economic status, gender and ethnicity.

Participants in each group filled out a survey before the group began, which recorded their attitudes and views in order to gain some quantitative data. Although the survey sample size from each area is too small to be anything other than indicative, the results are useful for immediate comparison between areas and to check the data trends against other polls.

Participants were asked to describe their feelings about living in their area at the beginning of the groups. This allowed ippr to place their later comments about asylum seekers within this context, particularly their views on the provision of public services. It also allowed participants time to discuss a reasonably neutral topic and to gain confidence within the group, before discussing more sensitive issues about asylum.

Groups lasted for one and a half hours, in different venues within each research area. Participants were recruited by an accredited market research recruitment agency, and paid a small incentive for attending the group. The groups were moderated by a trained ippr facilitator and notes were taken by another member of ippr staff. The sessions were also recorded to check the accuracy of notes and quotes. Discussions were standardised to allow analysis across the groups. A literature review of the academic theory was carried out after the key themes had been analysed, in order to place our work in a wider academic and policy context. Before publication an expert round-table was held to discuss the emerging findings of the research and policy implications (Annex 2).

Chapters two and three lay out key findings about what underpins attitudes to asylum seekers. Chapters four and five describe the main ways in which concerns are expressed, and explore what underpins them specifically. Chapter six offers some conclusions and suggestions for ways to move forwards.

2. Understanding attitudes: social class, knowledge and location

- The extent to which an individual perceives themselves to be at risk of economic threat is an important factor in shaping attitudes towards asylum seekers.

- Meaningful contact with asylum seekers, migrants and minority ethnic communities generally leads to more tolerant attitudes. Superficial contact can exacerbate prejudice and hostility.

- Local issues are very important in determining an individual's attitude towards asylum seekers.

- Widespread confusion about asylum exacerbates hostility.

Respondents' attitudes were complex and often contradictory, partly because this was the first opportunity that many had had to discuss these issues in any depth. There was a marked difference in the attitudes of the different social groups towards asylum seekers. Peoples attitudes also varied considerably between the different research areas.

The majority of all participants expressed hostile views about asylum seekers. Some were deeply opposed to any asylum seekers coming into Britain, while others took a more moderate but still largely hostile view. In some cases this extended to any non-white or non-British community. Discussion focused upon groups who could be immediately identified as different; no one raised issues about white immigration from countries such as Australia or the US. A significant minority of people felt that the UK should not have a responsibility towards asylum seekers, and should tackle domestic social problems as a priority. There was a striking lack of empathy in the language used to talk about asylum seekers.

Fears about asylum seekers can be broadly categorised as concerns about economic impacts (such as on the labour market or welfare systems) and about cultural and social change (such as increased racial diversity and overcrowding). Underlying these are fears that the asylum system is out of control and that the Government has failed to address the issue.

A small minority welcomed asylum seekers largely unreservedly. There was also considerable and broad support for the principle of asylum and for the UK's role in providing protection for those who are in need of it. This suggests that people are not necessarily opposed to the principle of providing protection to those who are in need of it. More than three quarters of those who participated in the research felt that people in fear of their lives should be allowed to remain in the UK. This reflects other research in which a similar proportion

(78 per cent) of the British public said that people fleeing from genocide or
ethnic cleansing should usually be allowed entry, or at least be given the right
to have their case judged on its merits (Joseph Rowntree Reform Trust, 2004).

There was also confusion over different kinds of migrants. This meant
that the discussions were rarely limited solely to issues associated with asylum seekers. Very few participants were able to distinguish confidently
between different categories of migrants. In some cases this meant any non-
white person was classed as an asylum seeker. White European migrants
were also often described as asylum seekers. There was also very little
knowledge about the numbers of asylum seekers or the relative proportion
that come to the UK, and both were greatly exaggerated.

We have developed a model to explain our findings. This attempts to
explain the relative importance of different factors in forming attitudes
towards asylum seekers. It shows the complex interaction between social
class, locality and the overall context of political and media discourse. All
these factors determine how people feel about asylum seekers. The model
shows that the degree to which someone is vulnerable to economic competition and the level of contact they have with people from a different economic background to themselves are critical in determining their attitudes.
Local issues are hugely important in establishing views.

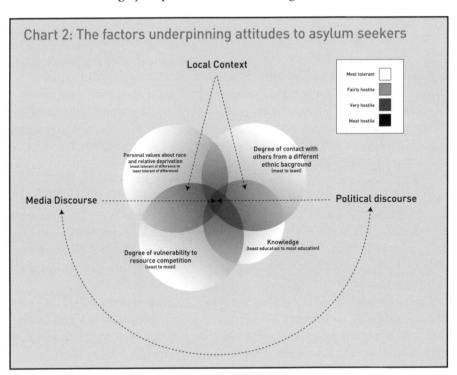

There is very little research or theoretical evidence on what factors influence
attitudes specifically towards asylum seekers as opposed to immigrants in gen-

eral. The analysis in this chapter and the next therefore largely draws on evidence about the factors shaping attitudes to other immigrant groups and minority ethnic communities more generally.

Table 2: Overall attitudes by social group	
Group	**Overall attitudes**
ABC1 25 to 50	This group was the most tolerant overall and generally well informed about the issues. Their views diverged; a substantial minority expressed positive views about asylum seekers and felt that the UK should be more welcoming. This group expressed concern about the hostile views they perceived the general public to hold. Many people questioned the degree of impact asylum seekers have, both locally and nationally.
	However, others held very negative attitudes about asylum seekers. They expressed concerns about the use of taxes to fund public services accessed by migrants and about social change and crime.
ABC1 51 and over	This group was more hostile than the younger ABC1 social group. They were particularly concerned about health services and house prices, and expressed some racist attitudes. These were often couched in terms of perceived negative cultural impacts.
C2DE 25 to 50	This group was largely hostile towards asylum seekers, and felt their impacts upon the economy to be significant. There was little knowledge about different groups of migrants and the legal status of asylum seekers. Most participants expressed fears about the impact of asylum seekers upon social housing, jobs and benefits, as well as a degree of concern about perceived negative impacts on British values and identity. Some overtly racist views were expressed, although many people said they were frustrated by the fact that any attempt to criticise asylum seekers was branded as racism.
C2DE 51 and over	The most hostile, and least well informed of all the groups. Many participants were anxious about the threat they perceived asylum seekers and immigration to pose to British values and identity. This was often

<table>
<tr><td></td><td>expressed in racist language. They were particularly concerned about the perceived impacts of asylum seekers on the availability of social housing.</td></tr>
<tr><td>17 to 19 year olds</td><td>This group had the most diverse views, with a fairly even split between extreme levels of hostility and a strongly expressed desire to welcome asylum seekers to the UK. These attitudes largely correlated with levels of education, with the more educated participants generally being more tolerant. The most commonly held anxieties stemmed from perceptions about having to compete for housing, benefits and jobs, and a sense that British identity and values are under threat.</td></tr>
<tr><td>BME groups</td><td>These groups were largely fairly tolerant of asylum seekers and well informed about the issues. Participants from established communities expressed fears that others assumed that they were asylum seekers. Tensions between different minority ethnic groups meant that not everyone felt empathy towards asylum seekers, but these participants were generally far more concerned about human rights. Concerns about asylum seekers were expressed in relation to their perceived impact upon services, jobs and housing, rather than about British social values or cultural impacts.</td></tr>
</table>

Individual characteristics

An individual's ethnicity, level of education and age are all likely to affect their views about asylum seekers.

Ethnic background

People from BME communities were less likely to display very overt hostility about asylum seekers, and more likely to express sympathy than their white counterparts. In particular many people related to the experience of immigration. This finding cut across social class. Nonetheless there was still a reasonably high degree of concern about asylum seekers, expressed in terms of economic threats. People with cultural and ethnic ties to immigrants might be expected to promote pro-immigrant attitudes and support for more open immigration policy but the fact that minority ethnic respondents are more likely to be economically marginalised can lead to contradictory results (Fetzer, 2000).

'Narrow minded people don't understand the differences between groups and think we're the same as them.' Male, BME, Birmingham.

Some people from a minority ethnic background were concerned that the focus on asylum seekers and immigration made them more vulnerable, and felt that it had increased intolerance and racism. This made them resentful of more recently arrived groups for undermining the status quo. Some believed the levels of economic support for immigrants to be greater than previously. This increased concern about the perceived economic impacts of asylum seekers.

Tensions between different minority ethnic groups also increased concern about asylum seekers. For example, in Birmingham shifting populations in particular areas are leading to tension between the Pakistani and Somali communities, which are being exploited by anti-immigration parties; the BNP has targeted British Hindu and Sikh communities by focusing on an anti-Muslim campaign.

A YouGov poll commissioned by the CRE (2004b) designed to identify differences in attitudes between white and non-white respondents found that white respondents were more hostile towards recent immigrants to Britain than non-white respondents. More than a quarter of the white respondents thought that the average white Briton is better or worse off than the average non-white person, whereas only 10 per cent of non-white respondents shared this view. As with ippr's research, the survey also suggested a considerable degree of hostility among existing minority ethnic communities towards asylum and immigration.

Education

There is evidence that differing levels of education play an important role in shaping attitudes towards migrants. People educated to tertiary level were more likely to think that asylum seekers and refugees have a positive impact or little impact on national and local employment. They were also significantly more likely than those only educated to secondary level to think that the most important reason why asylum seekers and refugees come to the UK is to escape persecution (in ippr's survey the percentage was 73 per cent compared with 47 per cent).

ippr's research found that people with higher levels of education were much more wary of the tabloid press than other groups. Their education has enabled them to analyse information, and has also given them a route into the kinds of jobs which are the least likely to be threatened by migrant labour. People with tertiary education may also be more likely to have attended a university with a more diverse population than their home town, and therefore have had meaningful contact with people from different ethnic backgrounds to themselves.

A number of surveys and opinion polls indicate that higher levels of education contribute to more positive attitudes towards immigration (see also Saggar and Drean, 2001). Dustmann and Preston found the strongest link to racial prejudice was education; highly educated people were ten to fifteen times less likely to express racially intolerant opinions than individuals with low education (Dustmann and Preston, 2000). Alarmingly, however, McLaren and Johnson found that the greatest increase in hostility towards immigrants over the last decade was among those with a university degree (McLaren and Johnson, 2004).

Age

There is some correlation between age and attitudes. Both the younger and older groups expressed very hostile views towards asylum seekers. Young people felt they were competing against newcomers to get a job or a home. Similarly, older people often felt they had to compete for welfare benefits and rights which previously they could take for granted. They were also likely to associate asylum seekers with what they perceived to be negative social change.

> *'We've known this country since we were kids and the change has been awful, including the break up of communities.'* Female, C2DE, 51 and over, Camden.

The relationship between age and attitudes may be strong because age is a direct measure of life experience, because it captures cohort effects (older people are less likely to have had contact with people from different ethnic backgrounds) and because age reflects an individual's position in his or her economic life cycle (Saggar and Drean, 2001 and Rothon and Heath, 2003).

Social class

ippr found that the more vulnerable someone feels to economic competition, the more likely they are to be concerned about asylum seekers and their apparent impacts on the economy. This is, largely, not driven by any actual impact, and concerns are expressed as strongly in areas with very few asylum seekers and immigrants as in those with higher numbers. Attitudes are very largely based on perceived economic consequences rather than actual knowledge or experience.

> *'I want to know if all the illegal immigrants weren't here how much better our NHS would be and how much better our education system would be and how much better our roads would be.'* Male, 17 to 19, Weymouth.

Economic interpretations of attitudes towards immigration dominate popular explanations of anti-immigrant sentiments and also many academic studies (Fetzer, 2000). These argue that opposition to immigration arises from economic deprivation and the fear of further financial decline, and that negative attitudes to immigration should be more pronounced for those who are most directly affected by the competition of migrant workers (especially when welfare concerns are also involved) (Dustmann and Preston, 2003).

Other versions of this theory suggest that the role of labour market position and income in shaping attitudes is more complicated. Both Fetzer (2000) and Dustmann and Preston (2003) argue that there are two aspects of the actual or perceived economic impact of immigration that need to be taken into account: the labour market and the use of publicly funded public services. These will have differing implications for different socio-economic groups. People concerned about the first issue fear that immigrants – often willing to work for less pay and to fill positions demanding fewer skills – will reduce the native-born working class's wages or take jobs. Those who worry about the second are usually contributing most through taxation to public services, and express concerns about welfare system use. ippr's research found that economic vulnerability is an important factor in individual attitudes to asylum seekers.

Personal values

An individual's views on race relations, social justice and Britain's place in the world shape their attitudes towards asylum seekers. Unsurprisingly people holding racist or highly nationalist views are hostile towards asylum seekers. This is discussed in detail in chapter 4.

There is a strong sense among the white population that white people are treated unfairly in relation to minority groups and that these groups – especially asylum seekers – are receiving preferential treatment. Relative deprivation offers a very useful framework for analysing these attitudes because it refers to 'a feeling of injustice when others receive more than they "should" in relation to their efforts, their needs, their rank etc, whether such a difference is based upon a real difference or an assumed one' (Hernes and Knudsen, 1992).

When others receive something they do not deserve or are perceived not to deserve – for example, they obtain certain benefits without working for them, or are given a status which they are not considered to be worthy of – people react negatively (Fetzer, 2000). ippr's research found that relative deprivation can produce discontent and anti-immigrant sentiment even where there is no evidence of an actual negative economic impact.

Knowledge about asylum

'You see them walking around the city, asylum seekers, although you can't be sure that they are. They look like them ... they've got beards and stuff. You notice there are more in town.' Male, 17 to 19, Norwich.

People who know a considerable amount about asylum tend to assume that the 'problem' is not particularly grave. However, it is difficult to work out the direct relationship with factors such as level of education and newspaper readership. ippr's analysis suggests that relatively small levels of knowledge are not enough to counter the other factors described above. Any discussion about knowledge immediately revealed very low levels of trust in most information sources (discussed in the next chapter).

Most people taking part in the focus group discussions admitted low levels of knowledge, yet held very strong views. Many were unwilling to hear facts from other participants which contradicted these views. There was significant confusion about different categories of migrants, the numbers of asylum seekers in the UK and the benefits received by asylum seekers. All non-white people, and/or white European migrants, were often described as asylum seekers.

There is a popular assumption that the vast majority of asylum seekers are not in fear of persecution and should not be claiming asylum. In part this stems from confusion over the legal status of an asylum seeker. Many people in the focus groups understood 'genuine' to refer to the way someone entered the UK. They therefore assumed that anyone entering 'illegally' (for example hidden in a lorry) is not a genuine asylum seeker. There was also generally poor knowledge about international issues. Virtually no participant mentioned events such as the wars in Iraq or Afghanistan as potential drivers of asylum.

'There's no distinction made between different kinds of immigrants and the Government doesn't give you information about policy'. Female, ABC1, 25 to 50, Camden.

Many research participants assumed that lack of knowledge is politically driven, and that the actual state of affairs is in fact worse than they have been led to believe. The majority of respondents (85 per cent) did not feel that they had enough information about asylum and refugee issues. Most did not think that the information they received was clear about the differences between different groups of immigrants. When asked to estimate how many asylum seekers or refugees lived in their area most participants either did not know or overestimated the numbers. Nearly one third of respondents in Norwich estimated that between 2,000 and 5,000 asylum seekers and refugees live in the city, and a few thought the numbers were over 50,000. The actual figure is less than 150 dispersed asylum seekers (NASS).

Other research similarly suggests considerable misconceptions about asylum seekers. People regularly overestimate the proportion of the population that consists of asylum seekers, refugees, migrants, and minority ethnic populations (Saggar and Drean, 2001). This is significant when the current debate and negative attitudes are expressed in terms of the scale of immigration to the UK and related to concerns about overpopulation and excessive demands on scarce resources.

Table 3: Overestimating the numbers of asylum seekers and other immigrants in the UK

In a poll conducted by MORI for the *Reader's Digest*, the average estimate of the size of the minority ethnic population in the UK was 26 per cent of the population. The figure at the time was around 9 per cent. (MORI, 2000)

An ICM poll for the *Guardian* conducted in May 2001 found that when asked to estimate the proportion of the population consisting of migrants and asylum seekers, the most frequent guess was 51 per cent, although the real situation was closer to 5 per cent (ICM, 2001). More than a quarter (27 per cent) of all respondents estimated that asylum seekers and immigrants constituted more than half the UK population.

The public also exaggerates the proportion of the world's asylum seekers and refugees in the UK. Although the UK hosts just 1.98 per cent of the world's asylum seekers and refugees, the public estimated a number ten times higher, believing on average that Britain hosts nearly a quarter of the world's refugees and asylum seekers (MORI, 2002).

There is widespread distrust and cynicism about official information sources (discussed in the next chapter), and personal experience was frequently mentioned as an important source of information. A significant proportion – around a third – of respondents indicated that they got their information on asylum issues from friends, family or neighbours and an even larger proportion (38 per cent) from what they see around them. This is concerning as events are interpreted in the light of personal prejudice and confusion about different immigrant communities.

Included in the anecdotes relayed by focus group participants in Norwich for example, were those of a friend who did not get the council house she wanted 'because of asylum seekers'; children being pushed in the street by 'foreigners'; a friend being turned away at the doctors because he was told it was an evening session for 'foreigners only'; and, in one instance, a teenage girl telling a first hand account of being attacked by a Portuguese man. People frequently described the impacts they perceived around them through anecdotes related to their own or friends' experiences.

Personal experience is difficult to challenge and these kinds of interactions are powerful, reinforcing prejudice within others. This is particularly the case when people in positions of authority give out negative information about the impacts of asylum seekers on the local area. This evidence echoes the research undertaken by Valentine and McDonald (2004), which found that by far the most important source of knowledge is local rumour and gossip.

Locality

These influences on attitudes are played out in the context of where an individual lives. Attitudes to asylum seekers are strongly influenced by an individual's immediate environment. They varied significantly in the different areas. Local social issues were very frequently blamed upon asylum seekers, even in areas with very few asylum seekers or other immigrants.

Table 4: Attitudes by local area

Area	Summary of attitudes
Birmingham	Respondents living in Birmingham had the most negative attitudes overall. There was considerable hostility to asylum seekers. Concerns centred on crime perceived to be committed by young men, who were believed to hang about in the city centre causing trouble; resentment over perceptions that asylum seekers were given unfairly prioritised access to services; and fears that British identity and values were being threatened by immigration.
Camden	There were fairly mixed perceptions about asylum seekers. A reasonably high number of people were either indifferent or welcoming, but others believed that asylum seekers were given preferential access to housing and cultural resources. Most respondents were nonetheless positive about Camden's diversity.
Cardiff	Attitudes to asylum seekers varied in Cardiff. Some people felt that asylum issues were not very significant locally, although there was some concern about potential future impacts. Others were angry about the negative impacts they believed asylum seekers to have on public services, jobs and crime. The detention of asylum seekers in Cardiff prison was the most significant local issue raised in the groups, with resentment focusing on the perceived plight of Welsh prisoners. People living in Cardiff were the least likely of any of the research areas to express fears about an erosion of British identity. This seemed to be the result of a more positive sense of Welsh identity, but also a pride in the city itself as a result of the recent regeneration.
Norwich	There was considerable hostility about asylum seekers in Norwich. This focused upon their perceived impact on employment, British values, crime and public services. There was a widespread assumption that the nearby Portuguese community are asylum seekers.
Weymouth	There were strong negative feelings largely as a result of discussion about the accommodation centre on Portland. Concerns in Weymouth focused upon housing, a sense of powerlessness and perceived cultural change.

One of the strongest location effects is the extent to which an individual has the opportunity to meet people from different ethnic backgrounds to themselves. People with few or no personal relationships with minority ethnic communities were more likely to express overtly negative or racist views about asylum seekers.

> *'My mum won't go down to the park, she's been there all her life but she feels threatened: there's people of a different skin colour.'* Male, ABC1, 25 to 50, Birmingham.

Attitudes were more positive in areas with larger numbers of asylum seekers, refugees and BME communities (Cardiff and Camden) than in places with small numbers of asylum seekers and migrants (Norwich and Weymouth). Birmingham was different from the other areas because although it has a long history or immigration and the highest minority ethnic population of all the research areas, the city is strongly residentially segregated.

Contact theory focuses on the distribution of immigrants in a neighbourhood or region and on how many and what kind of personal contacts an individual has with newcomers (Fetzer, 2000). There is a distinction between 'true acquaintance' (such as being a dinner guest in someone's home) and superficial or 'casual contact' (such as a passing acquaintance in the street). The first type of contact most often decreases prejudice, while the second seems more likely to increase it. Negative individual encounters tend to produce powerful negative generalisations, but positive encounters do not work in the same way (Valentine and McDonald, 2004).

> *'I think Weymouth could change in a bad way because once you've got a few you are bound to get more aren't you? You accumulate a lot more.'* Female, C2DE, 25 to 50, Weymouth.

There is also evidence from other research that regional and local differences in the minority ethnic proportion of the population are strongly correlated with attitudes towards immigration. For example a survey undertaken by MORI in 2003 (MORI, 2003) identified some key regional differences in attitudes. The North East, West Midlands and the South West showed the most opposition to multi-culturalism, immigration and asylum; London had the least opposition to these issues; and the remaining regions fell in between. MORI found that three quarters of people in London (75 per cent) agreed that it is good thing that Britain is a multi-cultural society, compared with just 39 per cent in the North East.

Table 5: Local demographics and variation in attitudes

Birmingham

Birmingham is home to almost one million inhabitants, and contains a well established BME population, which makes up nearly a third of the overall population. Integration is an issue of concern for Birmingham City Council as BME groups are not evenly distributed throughout the city and are over-represented in deprived areas.

Birmingham has experienced inward flows of immigration for the last two centuries, with a marked increase after the 1950s. The city has recently become home to asylum seekers from a number of countries, including Afghanistan, Iran, Kosovo and Somalia.

The combination of high minority ethnic population density with largely racially segregated housing means that fear of visible minorities is not offset by a large degree of meaningful contact with neighbours or other acquaintances. The National Front and BNP have been active in some areas. They have exploited tensions between different minority ethnic groups by leafleting Asian households.

Camden

Camden's population of 215,000 is composed of a very similar proportion of minority ethnic groups to that of Birmingham (27 per cent). Although minority ethnic communities are not entirely evenly distributed throughout the borough, and are disproportionately represented in the most disadvantaged wards, there is greater diversity across the area than in Birmingham.

Over 75 per cent of Camden residents have said that they enjoy the cultural diversity of Camden (Association of London Government annual survey 2004), and 65 per cent thought that there were good relations between ethnic and religious communities. Camden has a long history of welcoming refugees, and there has been leadership on this from the council. The scrutiny panel report (table 15) means that the council is aware of the problems refugees and asylum seekers face in integrating. Most young people spoke positively about their experiences of going to ethnically mixed schools. Camden's education team has done a lot of work with asylum seeking children and has good practice guidelines about integration into schools.

Cardiff

Cardiff has a population of around 300,000 and a long history of well established minority ethnic groups. These make up 8.4 per cent of the population. They tend to be concentrated in Riverside and Butetown, and are not that well spread out through the city. They also tend to be disproportionately represented in key poverty indices. Nonetheless, as with Camden, Cardiff's diversity is often viewed as a source of pride.

Norwich

'I was watching a programme about Bradford where they have a lot of trouble, racist attacks and stuff. I can imagine that happening here.' Male, C2DE, 25 to 50, Norwich.

In the 2001 census returns, 96.8 per cent of the population of Norwich was white. Foreign students at the university have increased the visibility of minority groups. Integration has posed a problem for Norwich; high levels of deprivation and a large majority white population has led to hostility to BME groups, asylum seekers and refugees.

Work by the Norwich and Norfolk Race Equality Council reveals that refugee and asylum seeker communities feel vulnerable, and migrants and minority ethnic communities complain of racism. Members of the Portuguese community living in and around Norwich are commonly assumed to be asylum seekers. There is a fear of increasing diversity totally at odds with the very small minority ethnic population currently living within Norwich.

Weymouth

Weymouth has a population of only 63,648 and contains a very small minority ethnic population (1.3 per cent), the lowest of all the areas examined. Dorset has not had a long history of immigration and is not ethnically diverse (99 per cent white). Dorset County Council has mainly worked with asylum seekers from Iraq, Iran and ex-Soviet states. The ethnic groups were deliberately limited, both to minimise language difficulties and to reduce their visibility.

Weymouth's identity as a tourist destination means that people there already feel that their town is 'taken over' for long periods of the year. This means that many participants felt that demographic change is inevitable. The National Front targeted Weymouth for a recruitment campaign recently.

3. Understanding attitudes: politics and the media

- The statements politicians make and the language they use form an important contribution to the public debate. This in turn is reflected in and influenced by what is reported in the media, as well as findings from opinion polls.

- The media has a complex relationship with public opinion. It affects the overall tone of the debate, but does not necessarily directly influence an individual's views.

The need for political leadership

'I want to trust the Government but you get told they massage the figures.' Female, C2DE, 51 and over, Cardiff.

Political discourse forms the backdrop against which public debate takes place. Politicians are an important source of facts and information, and can determine whether an issue is deemed to be a problem.

Asylum and immigration have been the subject of extensive political and policy debate and have rarely been out of the headlines since 1997. In many respects this is nothing new and reflects a history of politics around asylum and immigration that goes back at least as far as the immediate post-war period (Solomos, 2003).

The politics of asylum since 1997 have largely focused on tackling abuse of the asylum system and reducing the number of applications. This approach and the policy measures which have resulted have been reflected in media coverage which has – in large part – depicted the asylum system as out of control.

The Government has emphasised that it is tough on the issue of asylum and on illegal immigration to the UK. Numerous policies have been introduced to deal with the social and economic problems of minority communities and to address the discrimination experienced by people from minority ethnic communities across a wide range of sectors and services. There has also been explicit recognition of the contribution that economic migration can make to the UK economy in general and to particular sectors of the labour market in particular. At the same time however, the Government has been keen to emphasise that it has the asylum 'problem' under control.

This has resulted in a political debate which has been framed almost entirely in terms of the pull of the UK, the numbers claiming asylum and how to prevent abuse of the system. As Flynn (2003) notes, the public statements of ministers and other public commentators on immigration policy are replete with references to the existence of a 'legitimate public concern' over the volume and implications of immigration and, in particular, asylum. There has been rather less discussion or concern about the causes of forced migration or how to ensure that those who are in need of protection are able to access it. In particular politicians have been reticent about stating the legitimacy of providing protection to those who need it.

It is clear that messages from central government and the politics of asylum play an important role in setting the context within which information about local issues is interpreted (Bauer, Lofstrom and Zimmermann, 2001; Saggar and Drean, 2001). McLaren and Johnson's analysis (2004) of recent British Social Attitudes data leads them to the conclusion that the current political discourse around asylum best explains the increase in negative public attitudes. In particular, the discourse about managed migration appears to have been confusing to the public, which is not able to distinguish between different groups of migrants.

ippr found that these measures have fuelled public anxiety about the effectiveness of immigration controls and about the willingness of the Government to respond to their concerns. This has reinforced the perceived need to be seen to be tackling asylum. Most participants in the focus groups felt that the Government had not effectively tackled asylum issues. People described themselves as powerless bystanders, watching the situation unravel. This was increased by broad disengagement from and cynicism about the political process. Only five per cent of respondents said that national government was the information source they trusted most about asylum and 31 per cent said that this was the source they trusted least. There was little variation in these views between different areas.

There is considerable anger over the perceived failure of the Government to address the asylum issue. Government statements are widely disbelieved, or interpreted as an attempt to cover up a problem. It seems that harsh talking has not worked: each attempt to toughen up the language and system has led to a belief that the 'problem' is worse than acknowledged.

'I don't believe them [the Government]. The other day they said asylum seekers had gone down by 30 per cent, but I don't believe them.'
Participant, C2DE, Weymouth.

This report was written after the 2005 general election in which the Conservative party made immigration a central feature of its campaign. Our research suggests that this approach will reinforce fears and the belief that asylum is a significant problem. This will be worsened by the lack of overt refutation from central government. Far right-wing parties such as the

BNP also exploited local concerns and fears about the impacts of immigration and asylum. These parties are more active in areas of the country where there are few minority ethnic communities and very few asylum seekers. In such areas, for example Weymouth, there is limited meaningful contact with asylum seekers to counteract negative political messages. In the absence of positive central government messages there is no one to put the case for protection. When asked in the focus groups to think of any positive impacts from immigration, many people said that they had never even considered this before.

Local authorities and devolved administrations can have a significant impact upon the tone of the local debate. The two areas with the most positive overall attitudes towards asylum seekers – Cardiff and Camden – also have the strongest local leadership on the issue. For example, Camden is keen to celebrate the contribution that refugee communities have made to the area. In particular, it set up a scrutiny panel to examine refugee experience in the area (see table 15). This allowed Camden to understand the numbers of asylum seekers and refugees, and their diverse experiences of living in the area.

Table 6: Croeso y Cymru: Political leadership in the National Assembly for Wales

Edwina Hart, Minister for Social Justice and Regeneration, has made a number of statements and press releases encouraging more positive attitudes towards asylum seekers and refugees in Wales. The All Wales Refugee Policy Forum was launched in November 2003. The forum aims to assist refugees to integrate successfully in Wales and to promote a more positive image of refugees and asylum seekers as members of Welsh society. One of the forum's key objectives is to address public and media perceptions of asylum seekers and refugees, and it has agreed to undertake a national campaign to challenge negative stereotypes.

The Welsh Assembly's Race Equality Scheme is also a key strategic vehicle for addressing refugee and asylum seeker issues. It makes specific reference to the needs of refugees and asylum seekers as a priority area and recently published *Asylum Seekers and Refugees: Guidance for housing and related service providers in Wales*. Further information can be found on the Welsh National Assembly website at www.wales.gov.uk

---

However, even in these areas most people said they did not trust local government over asylum issues. In part this is because they assumed that local authorities have to do what central government tells them. Nonetheless a high proportion of people wanted more information from the local authority. This suggests that an open debate about local asylum issues might help to increase trust in local government on this issue.

'The council are just a puppet of government.' Male, 17 to 19, Birmingham.

Many participants did not know much about their local authority's responsibilities towards asylum seekers such as housing, education or community relations. This led them to feel that decisions are not being taken locally.

Does the media matter?

In recent years there has been a significant increase in the extent to which asylum issues have formed the basis of negative stories in the national press, particularly the tabloids. Although this increase in coverage is likely to be related in part at least to the actual numbers of immigrants entering and settling in the country, it has been disproportionate to the actual increase in numbers (McLaren and Johnson, 2004).

Stories in the media frame the public debate on asylum, but the direct impact is less clear. Assessing the precise impact of the media on people's understanding of the world and on their actions is very difficult because people often choose a newspaper which reflects their views (Greenslade, 2005 and McLaren and Johnson, 2004). ippr found that the media does impact on the public debate, but largely through spreading myths and misinformation rather than direct influence.

A number of recent research studies have examined the role of the media in shaping or influencing attitudes towards immigration issues.[1] They found that that the media can influence attitudes towards asylum seekers and refugees in several ways (Valentine and McDonald, 2004). The media sets the terms in which the public debate occurs and can provide the stories and material to justify prejudices. Examples and statistics outlined in the media are considered to be accurate and independent, which is particularly concerning because in reality media coverage is often far from accurate and may be deliberately misleading about the scale and impact of asylum. Research undertaken by Buchanan et al (2003) reveals that certain sections of the national press are guilty of:

- significantly confusing the terminology about asylum seekers, refugees and other migrants

- using provocative terminology, including meaningless and derogatory terms such as 'illegal refugee' and 'asylum cheat'

- relying heavily on government officials and politicians as well as Migration Watch UK as sources for news reports and opinion pieces

---

1   See, for example, Buchanan, Grillo and Threadgold T, 2003; Finney, 2003; Buchanan and Grillo, 2004; ICAR 2004.

- presenting inaccurate, misleading or at best decontextualised statistical information, which may be unsourced, exaggerated and contradictory

- providing images largely dominated by the stereotype of the 'threatening young male'.

This is of particular concern given the lack of understanding of different groups of migrants (and between migrants and settled minority ethnic communities). Valentine and McDonald (2004) also suggest that the media encourages latent feelings of anger and disgust, and a sense of powerless among 'white majority people' that there is nothing to be done about the issues that concern them.

> *'It's happening and I can't do anything about it.'* Female, ABC1, 51 and over, Birmingham.

Research participants expressed distrust of the national press, which was widely believed to be deeply biased. People were very suspicious of information coming from the press. This echoes MORI's finding that 75 per cent of British people do not trust the press (MORI, 2003a). Participants were particularly suspicious of the tabloids, saying they had an agenda to push. Even those most hostile towards asylum seekers said that they did not necessarily believe what the press said.

However this distrust needs to be treated with some care, as people often used the same language as the tabloid headlines, and frequently gave example of stories from the press. In the absence of countering information, what is said in the press has an important impact through: defining the terms of the debate; providing negative shorthand language (such as 'swamping'); increasing public tolerance of hostile language; and reinforcing the idea that there is a problem.

> *'I trust our local press because they just tell us the facts.'* Male, C2DE, 25 to 50, Birmingham)

Local newspapers are important sources of information on asylum issues. Nearly half the respondents (48 per cent) indicated that local newspapers provided them with some information. The local press was more trusted than the national press. As Finney (2003) suggests, local media outlets are closely linked with the communities they serve and are thus in a strong position to influence public opinion while also to some extent reflecting and representing it. Local media reports that a national issue has a local impact or significance can have a particularly strong impact on attitudes.

This can be seen in Weymouth where rumours of an asylum accommodation centre being established on Portland were started by the local newspaper (see table 7). They gained additional credence with reports of a similar accommodation centre proposal in Bicester. Local protests against this were widely covered in the national tabloid press and in television programmes.

As a result of this coverage people living in Weymouth became much more concerned about asylum issues. According to local police sources this was reflected in an increase in racist attacks on foreign students. The legacy is an abiding fear of asylum seekers being housed in Weymouth and considerable distrust of central government in relation to asylum issues. The absence of official reassurance increased the sense that decisions were being taken without local people being consulted and made people feel that the government was attempting to conceal a wider problem.

Table 7: Media coverage of the Portland accommodation centre

In mid-January 2003, the *Dorset Echo* 'exclusively revealed' that the Home Office was planning to build an asylum centre for 750 asylum seekers on Portland, using a site owned by Comer Homes. Comer Homes had purchased the site from the Ministry of Defence in July 2000 and then sought planning permission from Weymouth and Portland Borough Council to convert the block into luxury flats. It seems that the company then had difficulties converting the block. Comer Homes responded to a Home Office advertisement for sites that might be suitable to be converted into accommodation centres. This made its way to the local newspaper, sparking a barrage of local opposition. Following a heated public debate of more than 300 people in Portland, the block was set alight.

The Portland accommodation centre story was front page news for the Dorset Echo every day for more than two weeks.

Hundreds in protest over plans for asylum centre on Portland

The trial of the man who set fire to the block also made national news later in 2003.

It is important to understand the local context of this story in order to understand fully its impact on attitudes to asylum. Portland is not typical of the rest of Dorset. It has its own history and houses a prison and a young offenders' institute. This clearly influenced residents' feelings about hosting another institution, and meant that the story gathered an internal momentum which enabled local residents to express negative views about asylum issues more generally. These concerns were often framed in terms of the impact on local housing provision, reflecting a widespread concern about increasing house prices in the area more generally.

Local media coverage varies significantly between the different areas. Stories about asylum seekers in Birmingham have been largely negative, and focused upon the economic impacts. There were some more positive stories about individuals, but considerably fewer than negative ones. Norwich also has fairly mixed coverage, with the *Eastern Daily Press* tending to be very negative, and the *Norwich Evening News* providing a more balanced account of local asylum issues. Media coverage in Weymouth has been dominated by the story about the accommodation centre in Portland. The coverage in Camden is largely positive. The *Camden New Journal* is widely read, and with a few exceptions is sympathetic to asylum and refugee issues.

Coverage in Wales has largely been positive and balanced. This is partly the result of the work done by the Welsh Refugee Media Project, which has built up a close relationship with the local press (see table 16). The debates are still largely focused upon technical issues rather than personal stories, but there appear to be fewer inaccuracies than in any of the other research areas. Noticeably fewer myths about asylum seekers were in circulation in Cardiff.

The coverage in each area largely reflects the dominant overall attitudes. As with the national media, it is difficult to be conclusive about the extent to which the local press creates negative attitudes or reflects existing local concerns. Nonetheless, the experience in Wales suggests that where coverage is more positive this interacts with other factors to produce a generally more tolerant climate.

Participants said that their single most important source of information about asylum issues was national television. Four fifths of those who participated in the focus groups indicated that they got information about asylum issues from this source, with the figure rising to 92 per cent in Weymouth. However, the prevalence of certain language and repetition of tabloid stories indicate that the print media do have a role in information dissemination. Broadcast media was widely trusted as a source of information and is generally perceived to be fairly neutral, particularly the BBC radio and television news. However, some people criticised documentaries for being too sympathetic towards asylum seekers. Others cited examples of television coverage reinforcing their views by demonstrating that immigration is out of control. This was particularly the case with undercover documentaries. Television can be a very powerful shaper of attitudes precisely because it is deemed to be neutral.

4. Perceived economic injustice

- Prejudice against asylum seekers is often justified by referring to perceived, and greatly exaggerated, negative economic impacts.

- Asylum seekers are frequently blamed for broad social problems such as lack of affordable housing, pressure on health services and unemployment. Where there is a local problem with a service asylum seekers are often believed to have caused it.

- Powerful myths about the benefits asylum seekers receive circulate in the workplace, and are passed on by friends and family. There is a widespread belief that minority groups are given preferential treatment when accessing services.

There is considerable public concern about the impacts of asylum seekers on access to resources. Expressing fears about economic competition allowed some people to justify racial prejudice in apparently rational terms. However many others were genuinely fearful of losing hard-won resources. This was reinforced by the concept of relative deprivation outlined in chapter 2: people felt that others should not be entitled to particular resources. Even those who supported the principle of asylum did not necessarily believe that asylum seekers should receive equal treatment.

While the impact of asylum seekers upon these resources is hugely exaggerated in the public mind, inevitably there are actual impacts. The lack of honest discussion about this, together with the perceived inability of the élite to deal with the needs of vulnerable communities, has increased a deep well of public resentment.

ippr's focus groups suggest that people living in social housing, BME groups and young people are particularly concerned about the impact of asylum seekers upon employment, housing and welfare. People from higher income groups are concerned about the impacts they perceived asylum seekers to have on services such as education and health.

Welfare and services

Resentment over asylum seekers accessing services and jobs is exacerbated by a widely held belief that they, and other minority groups, are given preferential treatment and better benefits. Asylum seekers are widely believed to receive better welfare benefits than the white British-born population and to access the welfare system with greater ease. Unsurprisingly this causes considerable anger. This view was firmly held, even in areas such as Birmingham where minority ethnic groups are actually much more likely to be living in deprived areas.

> *'We don't get all that they get, they smoke Benson and Hedges and wear Nike trainers, we can't afford those things.'* Male, C2DE, 25 to 50, Norwich.

These beliefs are also reflected in other research. For example, 72 per cent of white respondents agreed that 'minority ethnic communities receive too much advice and support from the Government', and 66 per cent thought that 'too much is done to help immigrants' (MORI, 2000). This reveals a very deep rooted belief that only certain types of people are eligible to access state resources, and resentment of government support for immigrants (however settled).

This sense that minority ethnic groups are given priority in access to services is exacerbated by powerful and widely believed myths. Asylum seekers are believed to receive benefits including driving lessons, free bus passes and swimming lessons. Again there was a tendency to assume that anyone from a minority ethnic background was an asylum seeker, reinforcing the belief that vast numbers of asylum seekers are tapping into the benefits system.

> *'Most of them come here to get benefits. When I went to sign on I was the only white person in the office, it made me really angry.'* Female, C2DE, 25 to 50, Camden.

Participants' beliefs about the welfare state greatly influenced their views on asylum seekers accessing resources. People who believed that only those who put into the welfare system should gain from it were angry about asylum seekers accessing any resources at all. Some felt that even asylum seekers deemed to be genuine should not be allowed to access resources.

> *'I was visiting a relative, and was told she was only allowed two visitors to a bed. Then an ethnic family come in and the whole family was allowed to visit; they get special meals and special treatment.'* Female, C2DE, 51 and over, Birmingham.

Access to the NHS was assumed to be an important driver of immigration. Many people immediately linked health care to immigration and thought that asylum seekers have a detrimental impact upon the NHS. This was the case across all social groups. A total of 45 per cent of respondents thought that asylum seekers had a negative impact upon the health service. Only 17 per cent thought that the impacts might be positive.

> *'People come here with HIV, it costs £15,000 to treat on the NHS. That's mad. And then I have problems getting a doctor.'* Female, ABC1, 25 to 50, Camden.

Attitudes to asylum seekers and health were underpinned by a general sense that the UK was under strain. Most people agreed there have been improvements in recent years but were afraid of the situation deteriorating. This reflects other research which shows that public perceptions of service delivery appear to lag behind improvements in services (Sargeant and Brown, 2004). Specific local problems are linked to asylum seekers in the public mind. People living in areas where they felt that there were problems with the health service were more likely to link asylum seekers to health issues negatively than people in areas where they were broadly more positive about the health service.

'Would you call immigrant nurses asylum seekers?' Male, ABC1, 51 and over, Cardiff.

Widespread confusion between different groups of migrants meant that people mentioned a number of different issues relating to immigration and health. These included health tourism, overcrowded services and tropical diseases. It also meant that many people assumed that migrant workers within the NHS were asylum seekers. Most participants firmly believed that minority groups get priority treatment within the NHS, which greatly exacerbated resentment over access to health services.

'My best friend is a chiropodist and she virtually treats only asylum seekers. It makes her mad but there's nothing she can do about it.' Female, ABC1, 25 to 50, Birmingham.

Employment

One commonly held concern about immigration is that jobs are taken away from the native population. This sentiment is particularly strong in the UK where about half the British born population feels that migrants have an impact upon employment (Bauer, Lofstron and Zimmerman 2001). This is reflected in our survey data, which showed that 53 per cent thought that getting a job is either a very or quite important reason that asylum seekers come to the UK.

'I got married at the weekend and my husband doesn't have a job. It makes me really angry 'cos you go to the Job Centre and you have to queue behind six Portuguese people; you're competing with them for jobs. We've got a mortgage and a daughter to look after, we just can't afford it.' Female, C2DE, 25 to 50, Norwich.

Very few people knew that asylum seekers are not allowed to work, so discussions took place on a basis of confusion between asylum seekers, illegal immigrants and other migrant groups. This also fed into perceptions that asylum seekers are unwilling to work. There was a sense of anger that asylum seekers were not visibly supporting the economy through work; as one participant in Birmingham put it, 'you don't see the dustbin men or postmen who are asylum seekers'. There was a general assumption that asylum seekers are unskilled.

Asylum seekers and other immigrants are in an impossible bind in relation to employment – they will be perceived as taking jobs if they are employed or as scroungers if they are not allowed to work. This means that opinion is divided over the question of whether asylum seekers should be allowed to work. The survey shows that 51 per cent of people thought asylum seekers should be allowed to work, with 29 per cent saying they shouldn't and 19 per cent unsure. Some participants felt that British people are unwilling to take up low paid jobs, so migrants are needed to fill these.

> *'If they're going to come here to work hard that's one thing, but it's the people who just come and sponge everything that are the problem.'*
> Female, C2DE, 25 to 50, Cardiff.

Particular local employment issues are likely to be blamed upon asylum seekers. In Camden and Birmingham, where unemployment stands at 8.9 per cent and 9.1 per cent respectively (Office for National Statistics, 2004) against a national average of 5 per cent, there was particular concern about the impact of asylum seekers on the job market.

Unemployment in Cardiff sits at around the national average and people living in Cardiff were more likely to focus upon the positives of migrant labour than in other areas. This may be partly the result of Cardiff's regeneration plan, which enabled participants to feel fairly buoyant about the city's prospects.

> *'If I had a deep tan and spoke Portuguese, maybe I could get a job.'*
> Male, C2DE, 25 to 50, Norwich.

In Norwich the Portuguese migrants (virtually universally described as asylum seekers) working in the Bernard Matthews factory were widely regarded as having a negative impact on the local job market; despite the fact that they were recruited directly from overseas because local labour was unavailable, and a steady drop in unemployment levels to 3.8 per cent in February 2004 (Office for National Statistics, 2004).

In Weymouth the seasonal nature of much of the available work increases job insecurity. This has been exacerbated by the recent closure of the New Look factory, previously an important local employer. This has increased fears that asylum seekers will take jobs, despite the fact that unemployment is relatively low, at just below the national average.

Housing

> *'There's a five year waiting list for a house, but asylum seekers can get one tomorrow – 60 per cent of houses have been allocated to asylum seekers.'* Male, 17 to 19, Norwich.

Two national concerns – asylum seekers and housing – have become irrevocably linked in people's minds. Housing repeatedly came up as a significant issue of concern in the focus groups, with people describing private housing as increasingly unaffordable and social housing as increasingly unavailable. Asylum seekers were widely blamed for housing shortages. People expressed discomfort about asylum seekers accessing what is perceived to be a highly constrained resource; many did not feel that asylum seekers should be eligible to access public housing. There was little knowledge about what housing asylum seekers are entitled to, and a widespread belief that they are automatically housed by the local authority as a matter of priority.

Fears about access to housing and perceived links to asylum seekers were widespread, whatever the real situation. Even participants who acknowledged that few asylum seekers lived in their area still expressed fears that their housing situation could worsen as a result of asylum seekers arriving. Concern about housing went across all social classes. While few from the ABC1 social groups were concerned about social housing, several expressed fears about the impact of asylum seekers upon house prices, and about 'areas being brought down'.

'Asylum seekers aren't a problem in Bridgend, but they could creep out of places like Barry and Bridgend could be a target, like a hotel could be turned into a hostel.' Male, ABC1, 51 and over, Cardiff.

Table 8: Variations in housing availability and cost

Birmingham

'Asylum seekers get homes. Those homes should go to our children. My children can't get a home and have had to move to Wales. We've had to help our children out financially.' Female, C2DE, 51 and over, Birmingham.

Although house prices are slightly lower than the average in England and Wales, they have risen very rapidly – a 14.4 per cent increase from 2003 to 2004 – leaving a whole section of the population unable to access affordable housing. Housing tends to be segregated, with minority ethnic communities still living in the areas where migrants moved to in the 1950s when discrimination restricted access to housing. There is 60.4 per cent owner occupancy in Birmingham. Birmingham City Council is aware of the potential for negative attitudes towards asylum seekers. There is particular concern about perceived inequalities and resentment over housing, and asylum seekers have largely been housed in areas where high numbers of people from a minority ethnic background live, in an attempt to reduce their visibility and perceived impact.

In Birmingham NASS currently provides accommodation for around 2,500 asylum seekers and subsistence only support to a further 680. There was a firmly held belief that asylum seekers were responsible for the housing shortage.

Camden

Camden is experiencing considerable pressure on housing, with high house prices and a great demand for social housing. People with middle incomes felt particularly anxious, as they are neither eligible for social housing nor able to afford high private prices. There is a relatively high proportion of social housing, with 26 per cent of people living in accommodation rented from the council and 11.4 per cent living in accommodation rented from housing associations. Demand still far outstrips supply. There are 13,000 people on the housing register or awaiting transfer from unsuitable accommodation, with 2,000 homeless households in temporary accommodation.

In Camden, very few asylum seekers are directly housed by the local authority. This runs contrary to the general perception among participants in Camden, who believed that the local council houses all asylum seekers as a matter of priority. One reason for this may be that people granted refugee status are sometimes housed more quickly as a result of their individual situation. The asylum seeking and refugee community is estimated by the scrutiny panel (table 15) to be between 20,000 and 25,000. At the beginning of 2004 NASS provided subsistence only support to 340 asylum seekers, with a further 15 people in NASS accommodation.[1] The shortage of accommodation in Camden meant that the council housed asylum seekers outside the borough before the official dispersal policy began.

Cardiff

'The price of housing is really bad and it has gotten worse; it's good if you're older and you already have a place, but if you are younger it's much harder.' Female, 17 to 19, Cardiff.

Regeneration in Cardiff has led to expensive new developments. This is seen to be an important aspect of improving the city centre, but is also driving up house prices. The Cardiff housing needs survey suggested that minority ethnic groups are more likely to be living in unsuitable accommodation than white households (Cardiff County Council, 2002). There were 8,000 people on the housing waiting list in November 2003 and at that time 4.8 per cent of homeless applications were from refugees.

---

1 This section summarises the available statistics for each area. Data on housing is not that readily available, and we know it does not fully depict the reality, largely because of multiple occupancy. Nonetheless, the difference between the perceived impact of asylum seekers upon housing and the actual impact as far as we know it is very great.

Cardiff is currently home to a settled refugee population of over 6,000 people and also supports up to 1,600 asylum seekers under the dispersal programme. In 2001, NASS was supporting 1,193 applicants, plus 700 dependents in Cardiff. While few people in Cardiff thought asylum seekers had a significant impact upon housing, there was a reasonably widespread concern that the situation could deteriorate.

Norwich

Norwich was the last local authority to implement the right to buy policy, which has created an expectation that there should be reasonably available social housing. This has also resulted in a sudden recent decrease in the availability of social housing locally. There are currently around 7,000 people on the housing waiting list in Norwich and 31 per cent of all housing in Norwich is rented from the council.

Norwich began to receive and accommodate NASS supported asylum seekers in June 2003. Approximately 100 asylum seekers have been accommodated by Norfolk County Council in Norwich and King's Lynn, and there were about 40 unaccompanied children in the area. There are 220 beds available, but these are not all being used at the time of writing. Despite these small numbers, rumours circulated in Norwich at the time of dispersal about how tower blocks were going to be used to house asylum seekers, and participants expressed considerable resentment about the perceived allocation of social housing to asylum seekers.

Weymouth

Second home ownership in Dorset is four times the national average and 73 per cent of housing in Weymouth is owner occupied. This is driving up house prices in Weymouth. Average house prices have risen steeply in the last year, creating anxiety among younger people that they will not be able to get on the property ladder.

In Weymouth the numbers of dispersed asylum seekers is very small – around 100 in late 2004. Weymouth Council was clear at the outset of the dispersal programme that it would not house asylum seekers, so people were housed with private landlords or in a hotel. There was some anger about asylum seekers taking housing, but less than in the other areas.

'Their ways aren't ours ... they are taking our culture away, their culture isn't ours. They've destroyed our community.' Participant, C2DE, 51 and over, Camden.

Beliefs about an unfair prioritisation of resources were particularly marked in relation to housing. Many participants made a clear link between housing and other social issues and several people linked the break up of long-standing communities to poor housing availability. This was blamed explicitly on asylum seekers, who were believed to be able to establish vibrant community groups as a result of housing policy and the other benefits they allegedly receive.

Where do beliefs and myths about services come from?

'Our council actually pays asylum seekers and refugees to have driving lessons, they've sorted everyone out with cars.' Male, C2DE, 25 to 50, Birmingham.

Stories about the services that asylum seekers are believed to receive are circulated widely, through workplaces and socialising. Young people said that they heard about them from their parents. Some of these stories have a clear basis in fact. For example, in Birmingham, participants complained that there was a special queue for asylum seekers in the local post office. It is true that a different queue was set up in response to complaints about the time taken to provide asylum seekers with NASS benefits. However, this was interpreted as yet another example of asylum seekers' privileges.

'When I ask why it is taking so long for housing the council gives me a reply of "there are asylum seekers and refugees who are placed in the hotels and B and Bs and they need to be housed first because you already have shelter".' Female, BME, Camden.

Frontline service delivery staff are important sources of information. People deemed to be in authority are powerful figures, and the information they give out is widely believed. For example, a participant from the minority ethnic group in Norwich described how he had been told to pretend to be an asylum seeker by local job centre staff as he would then access benefits more quickly. This understandably made him very angry and resentful.

Several participants said that staff in housing offices had told them that asylum seekers were responsible for social housing shortages. To some extent this may be a result of the confusion between different groups; people who are granted leave to remain may be given priority housing as a result of their individual circumstances. This is particularly the case for homeless families.

In Birmingham, these messages also came from the local authority when a councillor blamed the housing shortage on asylum seekers. At a national level political messages have focused upon reducing the benefits available – for example through the voucher system – rather than making the case for state responsibility to those in need. This is reinforced by other political parties who focus heavily on the perceived economic impact of immigration upon public services. These messages reinforce prejudices rather than tapping into the goodwill the majority of the British public display towards 'genuine' asylum seekers.

The national press is behind many of these myths. Stories such as *'Fury at asylum seekers' free golf lessons'* (3 March 2002), and *'Asylum seeker? Doctor will see you first'* (1 September 2002), both from the *Daily Express*, bring these issues together in people's minds. Headlines are particularly important, as people see these even when they do not read the paper in question.

'It was in the local paper that they get free bus passes, whereas old people have to pay.' Male, 17 to 19, Birmingham.

Participants frequently referred to things they had witnessed themselves, or had been told about by a friend, colleague or relative. These stories had a powerful effect on the rest of the group, and were difficult to challenge. For instance, one woman said how a friend of hers had sold a car to an asylum seeker who had paid for it out of state benefits. When asked how she knew that this was the case she was unsure, but the story made a strong impression on the rest of the group, one of whom said that he had read about these things but never believed them until now.

5. Social change and racism

'They haven't got any respect for our country. They haven't got any respect for the English. Maybe it's their culture or their creed or whatever.' Male, C2DE, 25 to 50, Birmingham.

- Broad social changes are linked in the public mind to the perceived impacts of asylum seekers.

- Many white people feel that 'British' values and identity are threatened by immigration, to the extent that they describe feeling like a 'white minority'. This is used to justify attitudes towards asylum seekers.

- Attitudes towards asylum seekers and other immigrants are partly driven by racism. This threatens to undermine community cohesion. These views are less pronounced in areas where there is a significant level of contact between different ethnic groups.

'London must be terrible; 20 years ago it was Bradford. I know it's terrible to say but they are everywhere now. In certain schools there are very few whites.' Female, C2DE, 51 and over, Birmingham.

Cultural and social problems are frequently blamed on asylum seekers. Concern about the pace of social change underpins many negative attitudes towards asylum seekers and immigration. People associate negative cultural and social impacts with asylum seekers despite the limited impact asylum seekers have on these issues. These include a decrease in community cohesion, an apparent undermining of British identity, and population growth.

The majority of white participants felt that British identity is being placed under threat as a result of increased immigration, to the extent that many people describe a sense of being in a 'white minority.'

'They hang around in groups, usually the men.' Female, C2DE, 51 and over, Birmingham.

The widespread assumption that any non-white or obviously non-British person is an asylum seeker meant that the asylum issue was absorbed into a wider discussion about race, with racist language readily used about asylum seekers.

'They get everything, there's a Bangladeshi club at my son's school, but there's nothing for him... it's political correctness gone too far.' Female, C2DE, 25 to 50, Camden.

Although culture is not a resource in the sense discussed in the previous chapter, there is a perception that economic resources are available for the celebration of minority cultures – including those of the devolved regions – at the expense of traditional British (or more accurately English) culture and values. Participants frequently blamed this on political correctness, which is described as a means by which the white working class is prevented from expressing 'traditional' views. People from social classes C2DE and older participants felt this most keenly. This is perhaps not surprising, as these groups may have a particular vulnerability to community breakdown.

> *'Like the black music awards, for black people. You couldn't have the white music awards and say "this is music for white people".'* Male, C2DE, 25 to 50, Norwich.

Many white participants were indignant that minority ethnic groups did not 'make an effort' to fit in and retained their religious habits, dress and language.

> *'They still want to keep their cultures and their arranged marriages and all that, they don't want to integrate with the English.'* Male, C2DE, 25 to 50, Weymouth.

This was perceived as a threat to British culture and values, and also as a deliberate challenge to the British people (generally assumed to be white). Some felt that minorities invite resentment by making themselves conspicuous. Views about integration were also influenced by a perception that individuals from minority ethnic groups rebuffed attempts to get to know them. Participants told stories which depicted non-white people as pushy, thoughtless and with no interest in mixing. They also thought the inability to speak English showed a lack of integration.

> *'There is a black family who live next to me, and whenever you try to talk to them they always ignore you, they never talk. They don't mix because they don't want to.'* Female, C2DE, 51 and over, Cardiff.

People frequently expressed concerns about losing a straightforwardly British identity as a result of increased diversity. This was linked to a sense that a 'British way of life' is being undermined by immigration. Again, this was articulated in relation to race and assumed that all British people are white.

> *'I know this sounds awful but why can't they conform to our ways? They stick together and bring down an area.'* Female, ABC1, 51 and over, Birmingham.

> Table 9: Views about multiculturalism
>
> Despite opinion polls showing race and immigration to be of concern, most Britons (70 per cent) agree that 'it is a good thing that Britain is a multicultural society' (MORI 2003). Increasingly people believe that being British is not dependent upon being white (McLaren and Johnson: 2004). However, outside city centres there are few opportunities for people to get to know others from a different ethnic background to themselves. A YouGov survey conducted for the Commission for Racial Equality (YouGov 2004b) asked respondents to indicate the proportion of their close family and friends who were white or from minority ethnic communities. Of white respondents 54 per cent indicated that all their close friends were white. Only 1 per cent of white respondents had any close friends from minority ethnic communities. Among minority ethnic respondents there was a much more mixed picture.

'There are many areas where people don't speak English at all. That'll happen all over the country. We'll get squeezed out and there will be no more indigenous population. Some people don't feel at home in their own country.' Female, ABC1, 51 and over, Cardiff.

These concerns were often described in terms of population growth and a negative impact upon services. There was a fear that Britain would be unable to cope and a widespread sense that this is an island nation with clear limits to capacity, although the terms in which this was expressed varied according to the local demography. For example participants in Norwich assumed that their area was under threat from an encroaching tide of non-white immigration. Although Norwich is largely white, Norfolk is more diverse and this has created concern within Norfolk. Like the economic arguments discussed in the previous chapter, this argument about overcrowding tended to be presented as a rational – and therefore unassailable – fact, which was very difficult to challenge. The national press has also focused heavily upon population growth and overcrowding, with headlines dominated by words such as 'swamping' and 'wave'. These terms were extensively used by participants.

'The UK is not physically big enough to cope.' Male, ABC1, 25 to 50, Norwich.

Crime

Crime is another fear. Many white participants admitted to feeling afraid of visible minority ethnic groups. East European immigrants in particular were believed to be linked to prostitution and drugs. Some people felt that minority groups act in a deliberately threatening manner in order to intimidate others.

'When you have ethnic groups, the way they carry themselves, it's threatening, they do it deliberately.' Male ABC1, 25 to 50, Birmingham.

Others felt that the presence of non-white groups was in itself threatening. Increased global insecurity exacerbated this and Muslims, in particular, were associated with terrorism. In reality, very few participants mentioned personal experience of crime and none had been the victim of a crime committed by an asylum seeker. However, most were convinced that asylum seekers are heavily implicated in crime.

'Most of them have got a knife or a blade. They're brought up different to us. These Muslims, you can't keep having them, who's to know these asylum seekers aren't terrorists?' Male, C2DE, 25 to 50, Norwich.

Levels of recorded crime varied significantly between the areas where the research took place, and local concerns about crime informed fears about asylum seekers and crime. The local media played an important role in this. For example, in Birmingham there has been extensive coverage of various crimes (largely driving offences) believed to have been committed by asylum seekers. Participants from Birmingham frequently refers to these.

Young people were the most likely to think that asylum seekers increase crime (32 per cent), compared with 24 per cent of people aged 51 or over. This may reflect the disproportionate impact of crime on young people.

Table 10: Variations in crime levels
Birmingham

'I feel intimidated by going into town. I wouldn't let my daughter go there. They are very much in your face and bringing in a gangster culture.' Female, C2DE, 25 to 50, Birmingham.

Crime rates in Birmingham are higher than average, particularly for violent offences, which are 19.6 per 1,000 against the national average of 11.4 per 1000. The dominant concern in Birmingham is a visible group of young men in the city centre believed to be involved in criminal activity.

Camden

'A lot of drug trafficking and prostitution is driven by East Europeans.' Male, ABC1, 25 to 50, Camden.

Camden has the highest crime rate of any of our research areas, particularly for violent offences. The Camden annual resident survey 2004 showed that crime remains the primary concern of Camden's population. Many participants said they fear theft and assault, which they associated with East Europeans.

Cardiff

Cardiff has average levels of crime, yet asylum seekers were quite widely blamed. In particular participants expressed fears about gangs of asylum seekers in Riverside and Ely. Many mentioned the asylum seekers currently being held in Cardiff prison, assuming that they had been put there because they had committed criminal offence.

Norwich

'You've heard that the number of rapes in Dereham has gone up. Most of them are from the Portuguese.' Male, 17 to 19, Norwich.

Norwich has crime levels close to the national average and very few asylum seekers. They were however widely believed to cause crime. The Portuguese community in Norwich – generally believed to be asylum seekers by participants – was perceived to have brought about an increase in violence and sexual offences.

Weymouth

The crime levels in Weymouth are considerably lower than the national average. This has ensured that crime is not a dominant concern, and very little was said about crime in the focus groups.

How much is driven by racism?

The debate about attitudes to asylum seekers raises important questions about the extent to which hostility is driven by racism. This discussion has been dominated by accusations of racism from both sides: anti-immigration groups accuse others of stifling debate by using the race card (for example, one Conservative party slogan for the 2005 election ran 'It's not racist to impose limits on immigration'), while asylum rights groups argue that much anti-immigration sentiment is caused by racism.

ippr's research found that racism does often underpin discussions about the cultural and social impacts of asylum seekers. People use very derogatory language about asylum seekers, and make little attempt to distinguish between different groups. Constant use of the term 'asylum seeker' in the media and by politicians has also created the impression that they are a distinct group about whom it is acceptable to express extreme forms of prejudice. There appears to be very little social sanction against negative remarks about asylum seekers.

'I hate the way they all head to one area when they come in, I could go to a shop and be the only white person there. I wouldn't want them to be my neighbours, I'd hate it.' Female, ABC1, 51 and over, Birmingham.

'There was that boat full of refugees which the Australian government was going to blow up rather than let it land, which I think is right personally.' Male, C2DE, 25 to 50, Cardiff.

The race debate has become more complex as many asylum seekers are from groups considered to be white, such as Kosovars and Albanians. Much of the most extreme hostility in the groups was reserved for these people, with some participants arguing that this is not driven by racism because they are white. There is a strong association in the public mind between East Europeans and Gypsies, who remain one of the most vilified groups in the UK. This latent prejudice has been brought to the fore recently by the Conservative Party's discussion of Gypsy sites, and the associated 'Stamp on the Camps' campaign led by the *Sun* newspaper.

'You see those East Europeans hanging around the station, and we all know what they are, they're Gypsies.' Male, C2DE, 51 and over, Cardiff.

Table 11: Racism in the UK

The 2002 British Social Attitudes survey found that two thirds of the British public describe themselves as 'not prejudiced at all' compared with 29 per cent who describe themselves as 'a little prejudiced' and only 1.4 per cent who consider themselves to be 'very prejudiced'. However a significant proportion of respondents (42.8 per cent) thought there is more racial prejudice in Britain than there was five years ago (Rothon and Heath, 2003). As McLaren and Johnson suggest, it is important to look beyond self-rated racism at perceptions of racism in society more generally as people may be unwilling to denote themselves as prejudiced (2004).

How people feel about immigrants is strongly related to their nationality. A poll for the *Guardian* asked respondents how they would feel if asylum seekers from different countries were to come and live in their neighbourhoods (ICM, 2001). Results reveal very different attitudes to people of different nationalities (Saggar and Drean, 2001). Virtually all respondents said they would approve of white South African or Chinese asylum seekers coming to live in their neighbourhood. By contrast, all groups disapproved of Iraqi and Romanian asylum seekers.

Chart 3: Attitudes to immigrants from different countries (from Saggar and Drean, 2001)

	Sex		Age						Social Class				Region		
	Male	Female	18-24	25-34	35-44	45-54	65-64	65+	ABC1	C1	C2	DE	North	Midlands	South
White South African															
Approve	✓	✓	✓	✓	✓	✓	✓	✓	✓	✓	✓	✓	✓	✓	✓
Disapprove												✓			
Romanian															
Approve			✓												
Disapprove	✓	✓	✓	✓	✓	✓	✓	✓	✓	✓	✓	✓	✓	✓	✓
Afghan															
Approve			✓												
Disapprove	✓	✓		✓	✓	✓	✓	✓	✓	✓	✓	✓	✓	✓	✓
Iraqi															
Approve															
Disapprove	✓	✓	✓	✓	✓	✓	✓	✓	✓	✓	✓	✓	✓	✓	✓
Chinese															
Approve	✓	✓	✓	✓	✓	✓	✓	✓	✓	✓	✓	✓	✓	✓	✓
Disapprove								✓				✓			
Black African															
Approve			✓	✓	✓				✓	✓					✓
Disapprove	✓	✓				✓	✓	✓			✓	✓	✓	✓	✓

More recently similar questions about approval or disapproval of different nationalities moving into an area have been asked by YouGov on behalf of the *Economist* (YouGov 2004a). The survey found that while 85 per cent of respondents would approve of or not mind Australians moving into their area, the corresponding figure for black Africans was 39 per cent and 16 per cent for Iraqis.

> *'Enoch Powell had the right idea. They should have put a stop to it there and then.'* Female, C2DE, 51 and over, Cardiff.

People were open about their views on racism and asylum seekers. One set of people – mainly women and people from social classes ABC1 – said they found asylum seekers unacceptable, stressing the perceived negative impacts of asylum seekers on community cohesion.

> *'I consider myself not to be racist, but I do feel strongly about asylum seekers; my experiences with neighbours haven't been positive. I know this sounds selfish but I haven't found them pleasant.'* Female, C2DE, 25 to 50, Camden.

Another smaller group openly acknowledged that it had become more racist as a result of the debates about asylum seekers. This was often justified by mentioning community tensions and cultural impacts. These views were particularly apparent in places with poor integration such as Norwich and Birmingham, and were held mostly by younger men and older people living in social housing. Council staff in Norwich agreed that the debate over asylum had increased racism.

'You become more racist, you can't help it – they're just as racist as we are.' Male, 17 to 19, Birmingham.

Most participants expressed prejudiced views about asylum seekers, yet few were prepared to be this openly racist about other groups. The inability to distinguish between asylum seekers and other minority ethnic communities however meant that these views rapidly spilled over into descriptions of other groups. Valentine and McDonald (2004) have also found that prejudice against one group is often transposed onto another. This is particularly concerning as race related crime has recently increased, following years of decline.[1]

'There never was a problem with race in Cardiff, but now there are far more of them; it's a different world.' Female, C2DE, 51 and over, Cardiff.

Older people and less well educated people expressed the strongest views about the perceived social impacts of asylum seekers, often using racist language. Better educated participants were more guarded in their language, although when probed, many of the same attitudes were apparent. Participants from minority ethnic backgrounds were largely positive about the social contributions made by asylum seekers and other migrants, and did not tend to hold these fears. However tensions between different communities meant that some concerns were expressed, for example the Pakistani group in Birmingham felt that increasing numbers of Somalis had undermined the historically good relationship between minority ethnic groups in the city.

Table 12: Race and politics

Race relations policies in Britain have assumed that the aims of public policy are to encourage the integration of existing minorities by dealing with issues such as discrimination, education, social adjustment and welfare. Strict immigration controls have been widely viewed at both ends of the political spectrum as an essential pre-requisite for successful race relations policies for integrating Britain's own minorities (Spencer, 1998; Statham, 2002; Schuster and Solomos, 2004). As Spencer (1998) suggests, this approach is based on the widely-held assumption that the hostility which some white people feel towards minority ethnic communities would be exacerbated if they believed that their entry into the country was not

---

1 Racially aggravated harassment increased by 23 per cent between 2002/03 and 2003/04 while racially aggravated less serious wounding increased by 11 per cent over the same period (Home Office Statistical Bulletins: 2003/04)

effectively controlled. Thus the reiteration that immigration controls are effective is intended to reassure that section of public opinion that the number of immigrants will not rise more than is absolutely necessary.

Other political parties are an important part of this debate. For example the BNP has described Norwich as 'the last white bastion city in England' and according to some of those we spoke to in the city, the BNP and UKIP have manipulated the tensions involving Portuguese migrant workers in Thetford to argue against asylum and immigration. In Weymouth we were told that the BNP was also keen to lend its voice to opposition to the rumoured accommodation centre on Portland. In the Welsh context we learn that BNP support is high in rural counties where there is very little experience of the issues and very small minority ethnic ratios. There also seems to be right wing political opposition from the White Nationalist Party and National Front in Birmingham, which have exploited tensions and hostility arising from residential segregation and lack of meaningful contact.

Despite a very heavy emphasis upon immigration in the 2005 election campaign, the Conservative Party lost votes to the BNP. In the outer London constituency of Barking, the BNP won 17 per cent of the vote.

'I wouldn't go round Aston now. We play a game of "spot the white person".' Female, C2DE, 51 and over, Birmingham.

Personal experience is important. In line with the contact theory described in chapter 3, the extent to which someone has meaningful contact with people from different minority ethnic communities is very significant in shaping their attitudes towards race and social change. For example, in Norwich, despite the large white majority, people were anxious about changing demographics and did not necessarily have the levels of contact which would reassure them. The largely segregated housing situation in Birmingham meant that many participants did not have that much meaningful contact with people from different ethnic backgrounds from themselves.

People were quick to extrapolate from one negative encounter and to assume that this represented an entire group. Stories of people who said they moved out of areas such as London to 'get away from' minority ethnic communities also increased the sense of an enclave under siege. Although many of these assertions were driven by racism, they were very difficult to challenge as personal experiences are regarded as unquestionable truths.

The inability to distinguish between different groups meant that discussion of these issues was never solely about asylum seekers. Many people identified all minority ethnic communities as asylum seekers. Although other forms of racism are increasingly considered socially unacceptable, there is no social sanction against expressing extremely prejudiced and racist views about asylum seekers and these views can undermine hard won gains in community cohesion.

Conclusions and recommendations – ways forwards

'You never hear or consider the positives. There are positives of ethnic difference and that creates diversity. I get a different view; I teach in a multicultural school. I see how interesting it makes the schools. It's important for children to meet other types of people.' Male, ABC1, 25 to 50, Cardiff.

The Conservative Party's focus on immigration during the 2005 election did not bring victory. However, it helped to win seats from Labour, and looks as if it will set the tone of the public debate in the next term. Public concerns over a very broad range of social issues, from service delivery to the make up of British society, are firmly linked to asylum. Failure to disentangle these issues will have very serious consequences for the UK's race relations.

Moving the debate on is possible, but requires commitment from a wide range of stakeholders. No single factor accounts for the current level of hostility, and effecting change will be a complex process. However, political leadership is the most vital element in this process, and the Government needs to accept that the current debate is a threat to progressive politics.

Talking tough on immigration has reinforced the idea that asylum is a problem and has not served to reassure the public. Despite the fact that the numbers of asylum seekers have been substantially reduced, there is still a strong public perception that asylum is being badly managed. The evidence from our research shows that central government needs to be more aware that the public does not understand the distinction between 'good' (economic) immigration and 'bad' (asylum and irregular) immigration. Unless a more positive language can be found with which to talk about asylum the public will remain concerned both about the issue and about the Government's ability to deal with it.

There is political space for manoeuvre. Our research shows that most British people do think that the UK should continue to provide protection to those who need it. The problem is that they do not have a full comprehension of the numbers given leave to remain or much trust in the system to protect genuine asylum seekers and/or to remove people whose applications have failed. Increasing public confidence in the system is one part of this. But strengthening the system must go hand in hand with confident assertions about Britain's international obligations to asylum seekers and the rights of asylum seekers and refugees. Government needs to rehabilitate the concept of asylum, remind people why the 1951 Refugee Convention was written, and separate this from debates about economic immigration.

Local politics play a vital role. Where there has been local political leadership the tone of the debate is markedly more positive. Local leadership can greatly influence other important factors which influence attitudes, such as the local press and provision of public services.

A hostile and frequently inaccurate national press has served to create and reinforce the public perception that asylum seekers have a negative impact on the UK's economy and society. It legitimises existing hostility and creates an exaggerated fear of the impact of asylum seekers upon services and resources. The local press has an important role. Where local coverage is positive and focuses upon the experiences of individual asylum seekers it can strongly influence the tone of the debate.

In the absence of strong political leadership and a balanced media there is little scope for the public to be well informed about the issues. Confusion is rife. There are clear knowledge gaps in people's awareness of asylum issues.

Many people are enthusiastic about wanting to know more, and would like to get information they could rely upon, preferably from a source deemed to be neutral. There is a plethora of asylum fact sheets and myth-busting leaflets already available. These do not appear to have much of an impact upon the public debate, partly because they are not reaching the right people, partly because they are not necessarily trusted. They have frequently been seen as the whole solution rather than as a small part of it. Nonetheless, continuing to make sure that accurate information is in the public domain is important, although the extent to which knowledge by itself can challenge attitudes needs to be treated with caution.

People welcome the opportunity for discussion and enjoy having the time to debate these issues. Public discussion is an important way to challenge negative attitudes, particularly where asylum seekers themselves can have the opportunity to speak about their experiences.

Racism is a factor in the asylum debate. It only explicitly informs the views of a small minority of people but many others express quite extreme forms of prejudice against asylum seekers (often prefaced by a disclaimer along the lines of 'I'm not racist'). General confusion about different groups of immigrants and exaggeration of the numbers of asylum seekers mean that many people readily identify all minority groups as asylum seekers. Prejudice rapidly spills over from one group to another, particularly in discussions about the changing nature of British society.

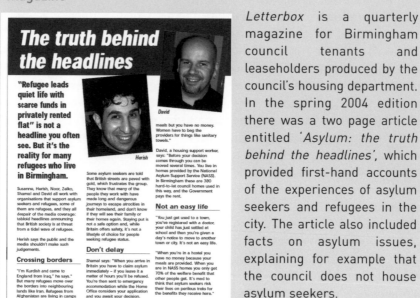

Table 13: Countering myths: Birmingham City Council's *Letterbox* magazine

The truth behind the headlines

"Refugee leads quiet life with scarce funds in privately rented flat" is not a headline you often see. But it's the reality for many refugees who live in Birmingham.

Susanne, Herish, Noor, Zeiko, Shamal and David all work with organisations that support asylum seekers and refugees, some of them are refugees, and they all despair of the media coverage: tabloid headlines announcing that British society is at threat from a tidal wave of refugees.

Herish says the public and the media shouldn't make such judgements.

Crossing borders

"I'm Kurdish and came to England from Iraq," he says. "But many refugees move over the borders into neighbouring lands like Iran. Refugees from Afghanistan are living in camps in Iran and Pakistan."

David

Herish

Some asylum seekers are told that British streets are paved with gold, which frustrates the group. They know that many of the people they work with have made long and dangerous journeys to escape atrocities in their homeland, and don't know if they will see their family or their homes again. Staying put is not a safe option and, while Britain offers safety, it's not a lifestyle of choice for people seeking refugee status.

Don't delay

Shamal says: "When you arrive in Britain you have to claim asylum immediately – if you leave it a matter of hours you'll be refused. You're then sent to emergency accommodation while the Home Office considers your application and you await your decision. During this time you're given

meals but you have no money. Women have to beg the providers for things like sanitary towels."

David, a housing support worker, says: "Before your decision comes through you can be moved several times. You live in homes provided by the National Asylum Support Service (NASS). In Birmingham these are 380 hard-to-let council homes used in this way, and the Government pays the rent.

Not an easy life

"You just get used to a town, you're registered with a doctor, your child has just settled at school and then you're given a day's notice to move to another town or city. It's not an easy life.

"When you're in a hostel you have no money because your meals are provided. When you are in NASS homes you only get 70% of the welfare benefit that other people get. It's mad to think that asylum seekers risk their lives on perilous treks for the benefits they receive here."

continued on page 12

11

Letterbox is a quarterly magazine for Birmingham council tenants and leaseholders produced by the council's housing department. In the spring 2004 edition there was a two page article entitled *'Asylum: the truth behind the headlines'*, which provided first-hand accounts of the experiences of asylum seekers and refugees in the city. The article also included facts on asylum issues, explaining for example that the council does not house asylum seekers.

Most people who are less positive towards minority groups do not regard themselves as prejudiced because they consider their views to be justified in either economic or cultural terms. The strong similarities in the negative attitudes articulated in different parts of the country imply that national level policies are important. At the same time however, perceptions of unfairness are also based upon subtly differing economic and cultural conditions. As such there is also a need for regionally and locally sensitive policies that challenge white majority anger and frustration.

People who have meaningful contact with different groups to themselves (not just asylum seekers, but also minority ethnic communities or religious minorities) are generally more inclined to be tolerant about asylum seekers. People who have either very little contact with people from different groups because they either live in predominantly white areas or in highly segregated areas are more likely to feel afraid and threatened when they see someone from a different ethnic background.

Increasing the levels of meaningful contact between asylum seekers and the settled community will begin to untangle the unpleasant strands of racism that allowed this prejudice to be so openly expressed. This is important even in places where the population is predominantly white. Clearly this sits within the long-term community cohesion and equality strategies, but certain specific actions can be taken to address meaningful contact between asylum seekers and members of the settled community, and to support asylum seekers to integrate more fully.[1]

Concern about having to compete for resources underpins much of the public debate. Asylum seekers are widely perceived to be responsible for housing shortages, for unemployment and for problems in accessing services such as health. The more socially vulnerable an individual is the more likely they are to feel anxious about the impacts of asylum seekers. These concerns are very largely based upon perceived rather than actual impacts, but they reflect the reality of social vulnerability. Unless attempts to address these fears are set in the context of a political commitment to tackle inequality and injustice they are unlikely to succeed. Tackling this therefore requires a commitment from policy makers to address social inequality and injustice as well as open up a debate about the disparity between the actual and perceived impacts of asylum seekers.

The bulk of this report has focused upon the role of politicians, the media and the local context in forming attitudes. In shifting the debate on, there is scope for a much wider range of bodies to be involved and the recommendations reflect this. However, political leadership at local and national levels is the most important element in addressing this issue.

Recommendations

Central government should:

- Openly discuss and affirm the UK's international obligations to asylum seekers and refugees, while ensuring that the asylum system works

- Openly refute inaccuracies in media reports of asylum issues

- Provide political leadership with strong statements on the rights of asylum seekers

- Support efforts to enable asylum seekers to integrate by offering English lessons (this may not be appropriate for all asylum seekers, for example those in fast track systems who are detained)

- Support a longitudinal qualitative study on attitudes to asylum seekers

- Ensure that staff in benefits offices have access to the correct information about benefits available to asylum seekers

---

1 The working definition of community cohesion is that of a society where:
   - there is a common vision and sense of belonging for all communities
   - the diversity of people's different background and circumstances are appreciated and positively valued
   - those from different backgrounds have similar life opportunities
   - strong and positive relationships are being developed between people from different backgrounds in the workplace, in schools and within neighbourhoods. (Local Government Association, *Guidance on Community Cohesion*: 2002)

- Improve the Home Office website to make up to date information easily accessible

- Improve information flows between relevant departments and local agencies.

NASS has an important role to play in preparing local communities for the arrival of asylum seekers. Providing accurate and comprehensive information and responding to the concerns of local people can help to reduce the anxiety that the arrival of asylum seekers can cause, and can also reduce community tension and the risk of asylum seekers being harassed.

NASS should:
- Avoid national dispersal arrangements which exacerbate integration problems, such as placing asylum seekers in very deprived areas

- Make empty housing stock available to other providers, in order to facilitate greater contact between asylum seekers and other groups

- Share good practice on holding discussions with local communities between different parts of NASS

- Provide more structured arrival support when asylum seekers are dispersed to a new area, for example by providing introductions to local communities

- Ensure that national information on asylum seekers is shared with consortia and local agencies to inform service planning

- Work with local authorities to ensure that 'host' communities receive some benefit from accepting asylum seekers to counter perceptions that asylum seekers get favourable treatment.

The CRE has a dual role of enforcing the Race Relations Act and changing social attitudes. As a result of the Race Relations (Amendment) Act, the CRE is working towards partnership with public bodies and developing a sense of a shared agenda. The challenge for the CRE is to get good practice and information on refugee and asylum issues to 'join up' with obligations under the Race Equality Duty.

The CRE should:
- Promote a balanced and informed public debate around asylum seekers and refugees

- Ensure that asylum seekers and refugee groups are considered alongside minority groups in relation to promoting equality and good race relations

- Identify, promote and mainstream best practice about integrating asylum seekers and refugees

- Examine the Race Relations (Amendment Act) in relation to its effectiveness in dealing with discrimination experienced by refugees and explore ways in which the Race Equality Duty could be used to secure improved outcomes for migrant communities.

Local government and devolved administrations should:
- Develop a coherent and overarching communications strategy about asylum seekers

- Ensure that obligations under the Race Relations (Amendment) Act are met by promoting good race relations

- Ensure that asylum seekers are included in evaluations of how effectively the equality standard for local government is being implemented

- Consult with refugee community organisations in developing race equality schemes and monitoring the impact of particular policies on asylum seekers and refugees

- Provide opportunities for people to get involved in more informed debates involving asylum seekers wherever possible

- Support asylum seekers to work on community projects or to undertake voluntary work while their cases are being heard

- Support museums and libraries to act as welcome centres where asylum seekers and other new arrivals can access information and meet local people, and also continue existing refugee work and arts projects

- Support refugee organisations to develop their capacity to work with local organisations such as schools and libraries

- Make information about asylum seekers and refugees available on their websites, and use opportunities such as housing newsletters to counter myths

- Ensure that frontline staff in housing offices, social services and customer service centres have the correct information about asylum seekers to counteract myths

- Improve their knowledge of who lives in or has recently moved into the area, the languages they speak and their housing and other needs.

> ### Table 14: London Borough of Camden's scrutiny panel
>
> In 2003 Camden Council undertook a nine-month scrutiny panel looking at the experiences of asylum seekers and refugees in the borough. The aim of the panel was to enable the local authority to get to grips with the real facts of asylum in this area. It featured cross-party participation and support for its findings.
>
> The panel decided to focus its efforts on examining access to further education, employment and training for refugees and asylum seekers in Camden. It considered oral and written evidence from councillors, council officers, voluntary sector groups, employers and individual refugees themselves. The panel attempted to get a clearer profile of Camden's refugee communities in terms of numbers, countries of origins and skills. The panel identified the lack of government data in this area as a problem that makes it very difficult for a local authority to provide services and reassure local people. The report has provided a crucial evidence base for successful applications for money from the Neighbourhood Renewal Fund and European Social Fund.

The Local Government Association should:

- Raise awareness with local authorities of the role they have to play in ensuring that they fulfil their obligations under the Race Relations (Amendment) Act and that this extends to new migrant groups, not only the established minorities

- Encourage local authorities to develop and provide effective mechanisms for sharing information with local people about asylum issues

- Encourage local authorities to share good practice about integrating asylum seekers and challenging prejudice

- Develop ways in which local authorities can get access to the information, advice, services and support they need to promote good race relations in their local areas.

All housing agencies should:

- Be aware of the existence of and needs of asylum seekers in their areas (including people in private accommodation)

- Provide a successful transition from NASS accommodation into long-term housing for accepted refugees

- Share and promote good practice

- Be encouraged to provide accommodation for asylum seekers in appropriate areas, and not just in hard to let properties.

The national print and broadcast media should:

- Abide by the guidelines set by the Press Complaints Commission

- Ensure that headlines in particular do not contain inaccurate or misleading terms

- Develop relationships with asylum and refugee organisations to ensure balanced coverage, and include asylum seekers themselves in coverage

- Permit journalists to adhere to the NUJ code of conduct

- Use the guide from Mediawise to ensure that terms used are appropriate (www.mediawise.org.uk)

- Experiment with innovative ways of engaging readers and viewers in debates.

Table 15: Press Complaints Commission (PCC) Guidance Note on Refugees and Asylum Seekers (October 2003)

The Commission is concerned that editors should ensure that their journalists covering these issues are mindful of the problems that can occur and take care to avoid misleading or distorted terminology. By way of example, as an 'asylum seeker' is someone currently seeking refugee status or humanitarian protection, there can be no such thing in law as an 'illegal asylum seeker'. A 'refugee' is someone who has fled their country in fear of their life, and may have been granted asylum under the 1951 Refugee Convention or someone who otherwise qualifies for Humanitarian Protection, Discretionary Leave or has been granted Exceptional Leave to Remain in the country. An asylum seeker can only become an 'illegal immigrant' if he or she remains in the UK after having failed to respond to a removal notice.

Those groups set up to support and advocate on behalf of refugees and asylum seekers can provide further clarification to journalists if required.

Editors are, of course, already aware that pejorative or irrelevant reference to a person's race, religion or nationality is already prohibited under Clause 13 (Discrimination) of the Code. Similarly, the Commission – in previous adjudications under Clause 1 (Accuracy) of the Code – has underlined the danger that inaccurate, misleading or distorted reporting may generate an atmosphere of fear and hostility that is not borne out by the facts.

Local press should:

- Include personal stories from asylum seekers and refugees

- Develop relationships with asylum and refugee organisations to ensure balanced coverage

- Use the PCC code of conduct.

Table 16: The Refugee Media Group in Wales

The Refugee Media Group in Wales (RMGW) was set up in 2000. In 2001 the group produced a report called *Welcome or Over-reaction? Refugees and Asylum Seekers in the Welsh Media* (Speers, 2001). The key findings showed that although the Welsh press had reported on asylum largely fairly, asylum seekers were given little opportunity to voice their views or tell their own stories. The report also found that communication between the media, local government, the Welsh Assembly, agencies, residents and asylum seekers needed to be improved so that correct information about asylum and dispersal was shared and used in the media.

Following the report the group appointed a full-time Asylum Media Co-ordinator who worked with local media, asylum seekers and refugees, local government and politicians to improve the accuracy and depth of media coverage. Work has actively involved asylum seekers and refugees in challenging media stereotypes by providing training which equips them with the skills and confidence to be able to engage the media directly rather than through a third party. Relationships have been developed with journalists in Wales, particularly with BBC Radio Wales, *South Wales Echo*, *Western Mail* and *Wales on Sunday*. Reporters are aware that RMGW is effectively acting as a watchdog to monitor them and are increasingly contacting the group for information and to organise interviews with asylum seekers and refugees.

Local race equality councils:

- Should work with the Information Centre about Asylum Seekers and Refugees in the UK (ICAR) to provide locally relevant information.

> ## Table 17: The work of Norfolk and Norwich Race Equality Council
>
> The NNREC is an independent charity in Norfolk which has been working on promoting good race relations in Norwich and Norfolk since 1993.
>
> In 1998 NNREC launched its Norfolk Roots of the Future project. This aims to celebrate the achievements of BMEcommunities in Norfolk, to increase public awareness about contributions from the BME communities to Norfolk life and economy and to challenge and dispel stereotypes about BME communities.
>
> NNREC's most recent report *Norfolk at Ease: A County with a Vision of Inclusive Communities* was published in March 2003. The report sets out the community cohesion priorities for Norwich and Norfolk and examines the role of local strategic partnerships in delivering change. It also provides concrete examples of equality work and education initiatives undertaken by local councils.

Other stakeholders

Unless there are more positive messages coming from government, the difference that other stakeholders can hope to make will be limited. However, as the national debate moves on there will be an increasingly important role for different organisations to take, particularly at the local level. These recommendations indicate some of the actions that will help move the debate on, rather than being comprehensive.

Voluntary sector organisations are in a strong position to do the kinds of grassroots work needed to tackle misunderstanding and prejudice about asylum seekers. They are also able to work with different organisations, so that members can make links with groups they do not usually encounter. Arts, sport and leisure services can engage all sections of the community and break down barriers that exist between them; marginalised groups are often more willing to use these services than take part in other activities. Cultural activities also provide an opportunity for joined up working with other public and voluntary sector agencies seeking to address social issues. Religious bodies are in a strong position to increase understanding towards asylum seekers.

Participants frequently expressed the desire for an independent information provider. However, ICAR already fulfils many of these functions. It is not widely publicly recognised, and there is scope to expand its role.

ICAR should:

- Work to raise its profile with the media so that journalists approach it for facts

- Promote the need for a longitudinal qualitative survey of attitudes

- The National Refugee Integration Forum should fund ICAR to develop its information resources and improve its marketing and dissemination strategies

---

Table 18: Information Centre about Asylum Seekers and Refugees in the UK (ICAR)

ICAR already undertakes many of the functions that were identified by our research participants as being useful and necessary to inform public debate and understanding of asylum issues. Its work includes producing up to date information about issues of current concern, encouraging better data collection, improving access to and sharing of information, collecting evidence and improving the flow of credible and authoritative information on refugees and asylum in the UK into the debate and into policy discussion and formation.

A useful additional function would be a longitudinal qualitative survey of attitudes to asylum seekers, refugees, migrants and minority ethnic communities. This would avoid over-reliance on opinion polls and survey data. It would provide a clearer picture of the levels of positive and/or negative attitudes towards these groups and the way these attitudes change over time and it would be helpful in identifying factors that affect people's attitudes towards minority ethnic communities in general and asylum seekers and migrants in particular.

Professional organisations and trades unions should:
- Discuss why they are hiring foreign labour openly with the local community, through employee networks, union membership and the local press

- Ensure that frontline staff have access to information about services available to asylum seekers – for example by producing a similar leaflet to the Wales TUC outlining facts about asylum seekers

- Use the opportunities afforded by the five-year plan to hold discussions about economic migrants.

Voluntary organisations should:
- Set up links between different organisations so that members can meet informally – for example, organisations working with older people could link up with organisations working with refugee children and young people

- Provide opportunities for discussion about asylum issues, and make information available to members

- Ensure that staff have the information they need to counter myths

- Link organisations concerned with asylum and human rights issues with schools and other educational establishments to provide educational material that fulfils curriculum requirements

- Make links with faith based communities as well as religious establishments to provide resources to be used by their members or congregants.

Table 19: Increasing cohesion: Arts and museums

Celebrating Sanctuary (Birmingham)

Celebrating Sanctuary is a free open-air cultural festival that takes place every year in Birmingham. It celebrates refugees from all over the world who have made the city their home. Celebrating Sanctuary offers people the chance to enjoy the different cultures refugees bring to Birmingham and helps people understand why people are forced to flee their countries. The cultural, artistic and educational events that take place around the city involve refugee community organisations, arts centres, libraries, city council bodies and local voluntary sector organisations. Local libraries mount displays of literature from countries around the world that are represented amongst the refugee communities.

The Museum of Immigration and Diversity

The Museum of Immigration and Diversity is a permanent exhibition and educational resource based in east London telling the stories of the many diverse peoples and cultures who created British society. The widely acclaimed exhibition 'Suitcases and Sanctuary' was made largely by local schoolchildren who worked with actors, poets and artists. For more information see www.19princeletstreet.org.uk/

ALM London

Archives, Libraries and Museums London (ALM London) is the strategic development agency for archives, libraries and museums in London. It works to ensure that the unique cultural, knowledge and learning resources of London's archives, libraries and museums are made accessible for the benefit of all Londoners. Cultural diversity is one of ALM London's key priorities and is close to the heart of London's communities. In July 2004 ALM London held a conference on 'Enriching Communities: How libraries, museums and archives can work with asylum seekers and refugees.' The aim of the conference was to look at how archives, libraries and museums could address the needs of asylum seekers and refugees. The report of the conference is available online at www.almlondon.org.uk/uploads/documents/Enriching_Communities_-_final.pdf

Schools should:

- Work with local refugee organisations to provide 'real life' stories

- Incorporate materials discussing immigration into citizenship classes

- Use material such as those provided by the Jewish Council on Racial Equality to challenge racism and to discuss the experience of migration

- Treat prejudice against asylum seeking pupils as racism.

Religious bodies should:

- Overtly tackle racial prejudice amongst congregants, by publishing strong statements – for example the pre-election briefing on the BNP published by the Churches' Commission for Racial Justice

- Establish links between different faith groups and make joint statements about the rights of asylum seekers.

Table 20: Joint letter published in the *Guardian*

The Guardian Friday May 6 2005 **27**

Human rights must stay at the forefront

Geoffrey Robertson (Humanity's core principle is not safe in their hands, April 30) is right to remind us about the consequences if Britain withdraws from the 1951 Geneva convention. He is also correct in questioning the paucity of responses from religious leaders generally. But faith communities have not been silent. You recently published a joint statement on the importance of upholding the convention from the Jewish Council for Racial Equality, Muslim Parliament for Great Britain and the Churches Commission for Racial Justice (April 5).

Since the convention was a response to the Holocaust, the Jewish community, in particular, belongs in the forefront of the campaign to save the convention and reactivate a positive agenda on the rights of refugees. Whatever the out-come of the election, much damage has already been done to the integrity of the asylum system. Today people need more, not less, protection; the 1951 convention should still be the instrument that provides it.

Dr Edie Friedman
Jewish Council for Racial Equality
Antony Lerman
Jewish Forum for Human Rights and Justic

References and bibliography

Amnesty International (2004) *Refugees and Asylum Seekers: Northern Ireland Youth Attitudes Survey*: www.amnesty.org.uk/images/ul/a/attitudes.pdf

Audit Commission (2000) *Another Country: Implementing dispersal under the Immigration and Asylum Act* 1999, London: Audit Commission: www.audit-commission.gov.uk/Products/NATIONAL-REPORT/D9E27097-6916-4F34-A79F-B09BDA0ED352/anothercountry.pdf

Bauer TK, Lofstrom, M and Zimmermann KF (2001) *Immigration Policy, Assimilation of Immigrants and Natives' Sentiments towards Immigrants: Evidence from 12 OECD-countries*, Working paper 33, San Diego: University of California: www.ccis-ucsd.org/PUBLICATIONS/wrkg33.pdf

Blommaert J and Verschueren J (1998) *Debating Diversity: Analysing the discourse of tolerance*, London: Routledge

Buchanan S (2003) *What's the Story: Sangatte: A case study of media coverage of asylum and refugee issues*, London: Article 19

Buchanan S and Grillo B (2004) 'What's the story? Reporting of asylum in the British media', *Forced Migration Review* 19, 41-43

Buchanan S, Grillo B and Threadgold T (2003) *What's the Story? Results from research into media coverage of refugees and asylum seekers in the UK*, London: Article 19

Butler TS (2001) *The Middle Classes and the Future of London*: www.data-archive.ac.uk/doc/4400/mrdoc/pdf/a4400uab.pdf

Cardiff County Council (2002) *Housing Needs Survey* www.cardiff.gov.uk/Reports/Housing_Needs_Summary.pdf

Daily Express (2002a) 'Fury at asylum seekers' free golf lessons', 3 March

Daily Express (2002b) 'Asylum seeker? Doctor will see you first', 1 September

D'Onofrio L and Munk K (2004) *Understanding the Stranger*, London: ICAR: www.icar.org.uk/pdf/uts003.pdf

Dustmann C, Francesca F and Preston I (2004) 'Racial harassment, ethnic concentrations and economic conditions' *CReAM Discussion Paper Series* CDP 05/04: www.econ.ucl.ac.uk/cream

Dustmann C and Preston I (2003) *Racial and Economic Factors in Attitudes to Immigration*: doku.iab.de/grauepap/2003/coll_dustmann.pdf

Dustmann C and Preston I (2000) 'Attitudes to minority ethnic communities, ethnic context and location decisions', *Economic Journal* 111 (470), 353-393

ERCOMER (2002) *Racism and Cultural Diversity in the Mass Media*, Vienna: ERCOMER

European Commission (2004) *Flash Eurobarometer 155: Justice and Home Affairs*: europa.eu.int/comm/public_opinion/flash/fl155_report_en.pdf

European Commission (2003) *European Citizens and Freedom, Security and Justice: Qualitative survey of citizens of the 15 Member States and the 13 applicant countries*: europa.eu.int/comm/justice_home/doc_centre/intro/docs/eurobaro_qualitatif_en.pdf

Fetzer JS (2000) *Public Attitudes toward Immigration in the United States, France and Germany*, Cambridge: Cambridge University Press

Finney N (2003) *The Challenge of Reporting Refugees and Asylum Seekers*, London: ICAR: www.icar.org.uk/pdf/pubram001.pdf

Flynn D (2003) *Tough as Old Boots? Asylum, immigration and the paradox of New Labour policy*, London: JCWI: www.jcwi.org.uk/publications/IRPpamphlet1.pdf

Ford R (2004) 'Local diversity, prejudice and white majority welfare attitudes in the UK', unpublished MSc dissertation: www.sociology.ox.ac.uk/admin/ford.pdf

Glendall P and Hoek J (2002) *A Question of Wording*, SySurvey White Paper: www.sysurvey.com/tips/wording.htm

Greenslade R, (2005) *Seeking Scapegoats: The coverage of asylum in the UK press*, Asylum and Migration Working Paper 5, London: ippr

Hainmueller J and Hiscox MJ (2004) *Educated Preferences: Explaining attitudes toward immigration in Europe*: www.people.fas.harvard.edu/~hiscox/HainmuellerHiscoxAPSA.pdf

Hernes G and Knudsen K (1992) 'Norwegians' attitudes towards new immigrants', *Acta Sociologica* 35: 123-139

Home Office Statistical Bulletins (2003/04) *Crime in England and Wales*, www.homeoffice.gov.uk/rds/pdfs04/hosb1004.pdf

ICAR (2004) *Media Image, Community Impact: Assessing the impact of media and political images of refugees and asylum seekers on community relations in London*, London: ICAR and GLA: www.icar.org.uk/pdf/mici004.pdf

ICM (2001) *Asylum Seekers Poll*: www.icmresearch.co.uk/reviews/2001/guardian-asylum-poll-may-2001.htm

Joseph Rowntree Reform Trust (2004) *State of the Nation Poll*, www.jrrt.org.uk/FINDINGS.pdf

Koopmans R and Statham P (eds) (2000) *Challenging Immigration and Ethnic Relations Politics: Comparative European perspectives*, Oxford: Oxford University Press

Lahav G (2004) *Immigration and Politics in the New Europe: Reinvesting Borders*, Cambridge: Cambridge University Press

London Borough of Camden (2003) *Working with Refugees: Report of the Scrutiny Panel looking at Further Education, employment and training opportunities for refugees in Camden*: London Borough of Camden: www.cfps.org.uk/pdf/review/239.pdf

McLaren LM (2004) *Others from within, others from without: Attitudes towards EU and non-EU* http://:epop2004.politics.ox.ac.uk/materials/McLaren.pdf

McLaren L and Johnson M (2004) 'Understanding the rising tide of anti-immigrant sentiment' in Park A et al (eds) *British Social Attitudes: The 21st Report*, London: Sage Publications

Migration Watch (2005) *Opinion Poll on Asylum and Immigration* http://www.migrationwatchuk.org/poll_results_2005.asp

MORI (2004) MORI *Political Monitor: Recent Trends: The most important issues facing Britain today*, London: MORI: www.mori.com/polls/trends/issues12.shtml

MORI (2003) *British Views on Immigration*, London: MORI: www.mori.com/polls/2003/migration.shtml

MORI (2003a) *Trust in British Institutions: Report for the Audit Commission*, London: MORI: www.mori.com/sri/pdf/final.pdf

MORI (2002) *Attitudes to Asylum Seekers for 'Refugee Week'*www.mori.com/polls/2002/refugee.shtml

MORI (2000) *Britain Today – Are We an Intolerant Nation?*: www.mori.com/polls/2000/rd-july.shtml

Office for National Statistics (2004) *Annual Local Area Labour Force Survey Data* www.statistics.gov.uk/llfs/default.asp

O'Rourke K and Sinnott R (2004) 'The determinants of individual attitudes towards immigration' *Trinity Economics Paper 2*, Dublin: Trinity College

Page B (2004) *The Second Death of Liberal England?*, London: MORI: www.mori.com/pubinfo/bp/the-second-death-of-liberal-england.shtml

Palmer DL (1998) *Attitudes Towards Immigration in Vancouver*, Canada: Citizenship and Immigration Department www.cic.gc.ca/english/research/papers/perceptions.html

Quillian L (1995) 'Prejudice as a response to perceived group threat: population composition and anti-immigrant and racial prejudice in Europe', *American Sociological Review* 60: 568-611

Refugee Council (2002) *Attitudes towards Refugees and Asylum Seekers: A Survey of Public Opinion Research Study Conducted for Refugee Week*: www.refugeecouncil.org.uk/downloads/mori_report.pdf

Rothon C and Heath A (2003) 'Trends in racial prejudice' in Park A et al (eds) *British Social Attitudes: The 20th Report*, London: Sage Publications

Saggar S (2004) 'Immigration and the politics of public opinion in Britain', *Political Quarterly 74 (1): 178-194*

Saggar S and Drean J (2001) *British Public Attitudes and Minority Ethnic Communities*, London: Cabinet Office Performance and Innovation Unit: www.strategy.gov.uk/files/british.pdf

Sanoussi B et al (1998) *Determinants of Attitudes towards Immigration: A Trade Theoretic Approach*, London: Centre for Economic Policy Research

Sargeant R and Brown A (2004) Perceptions of Delivery: Exploring ways to build a more positive experience of delivery among the public: No 10 unpublished paper

Schuster L and Solomos J (2004) 'Race, immigration and asylum: New Labour's agenda and its consequences' *Ethnicities* 4(2) 267-300

Singh G et al (2003) 'Perceptions of racial prejudice and discrimination in England and Wales' in C Attwood et al *2001 Citizenship Survey: People, families and communities*, London: Home Office: www.homeoffice.gov.uk/rds/pdfs2/hors270.pdf

Solomos J (2003) *Race and Racism in Britain* (edition 3), Basingstoke: Palgrave Macmillan

Speers T (2001) *Welcome or Over-reaction? Refugees and asylum seekers in the Welsh media*, Cardiff: Wales Media Forum

Spencer S (ed) (2003) *The Politics of Migration: Managing Opportunity, Conflict and Change*, London: Blackwell

Spencer S (1998) 'The impact of immigration policy on race relations' in Blackstone T et al (eds) *Race Relations in Britain: A developing agenda*, London: Routledge

Statham, P (2001) *State Policies, Political Discourse and 'White' Public Opinion on Ethnic Relations and Immigration in Britain: Pushing the borders of 'extremity'?*: www.essex.ac.uk/ECPR/events/jointsessions/paperarchive/grenoble/ws14/statham.pdf

Statham P (2002) 'The Contentious Politics of Asylum in Britain and Europe: A Research Outline', *European Political Communications Working Paper Series* issue 1/02: http://ics.leeds.ac.uk/eurpolcom/exhibits/paper1.pdf

Stonewall (2003) *Profiles of Prejudice – The Nature of Prejudice in England: In-depth analysis of findings*, London: Stonewall: www.stonewall.org.uk/docs/finalpop.pdf

The Sun (2003) 'Halt the Asylum Tide Now', 18 August

Thalhammer E et al (2001) *Attitudes towards Minority Groups in the European Union: A special analysis of the Eurobarometer survey on behalf of the European Monitoring Centre on Race and Xenophobia*, Vienna: SORA: europa.eu.int/comm/public_opinion/archives/ebs/ebs_138_tech.pdf

Thomson M (2003) 'Images of Sangatte: political representations of asylum seeking in France and the UK', *Sussex Immigration Working Paper 18*, Brighton: University of Sussex:
www.sussex.ac.uk/migration/publications/working_papers/mwp18.pdf

Tilley J, Exley S and Heath A (2004) 'Dimensions of British identity' in Park A et al (eds) *British Social Attitudes*: The 21st Report, London: Sage Publications

Valentine G and McDonald I (2004) *Understanding Prejudice: Attitudes towards minorities*, London: Stonewall:
www.stonewall.org.uk/docs/Understanding_Prejudice.pdf

YouGov (2004a) *Survey on Attitudes to Immigration*:
www.yougov.co.uk/yougov_website/asp_besPollArchives/pdf/OMI040101093_1.pdf

YouGov (2004b) *Survey on Racial Equality*:
www.yougov.co.uk/yougov_website/asp_besPollArchives/pdf/RCF040101001_1.pdf

YouGov (2003) *Survey on Immigration and Asylum*:
www.yougov.co.uk/yougov_website/asp_besPollArchives/pdf/TSU030101001.pdf

Annex 1. List of interviewees

George Binette	Equality Officer, Camden Council
Vanessa Buccoli	Refugee Media Group in Wales, Cardiff
Helen Buhaenko	Oxfam, Cardiff
Peter Bury	Environmental Health Department, Weymouth and Portland Borough Council
Bridget Buttinger	Organisational Development, Norwich City Council
Theresa Clemens	NASS (South West)
Nicola Cole	Housing Department, Cardiff City Council
Hereward Cooke	Local councillor and Chairman of the Multi-Agency Group, Norwich
Workneh Dechasa	Refugee Education Project, Local Education Authority, Camden
Adam Demosthenous	Building Stronger Communities Team, Camden Council
Heather Fallows	Local artist, Dorset
David Farnsworth	Welsh Refugee Council, Cardiff
Peter Farrell	Local and county councillor, Weymouth and Dorset
Dean Flowers	NASS (South West)
Julian Foster	Central Norwich Citizens Forum
Victoria Harkness	Scrutiny Committee, Camden Council
Barbara Hart	Minority Ethnic Achievement Service, Dorset
Glenda Gallacher	Asylum Seekers Team, Social Services, Camden
Sue Gee	Norwich Social Services
Cilla Lynch	Asylum Seekers Team, Dorset County Council
Anne Matin	Norfolk and Norwich Race Equality Council
Stuart Mudie	Housing Department, Norwich City Council
David Murdock	*Dorset Echo*
Zahid Noor	Welsh Refugee Council, Cardiff
Adrian Randall	Asylum Housing Team, Birmingham City Council
Mark Rawlins	Weymouth Community College
Ricky Romain	Local artist, Dorset
Mohan Sandhar	Equalities Manager, Birmingham City Council
Vickie Skade	Scrutiny Committee, Camden Council
Samire Shokry	Red Cross Asylum Seeker Drop-In Centre, Norwich

Michael Scorer	Housing – Needs and Access, Camden Council
Terry Threadgold	University of Wales, Cardiff
Andy Vickers	Dorset County Council
Monica Vidal	Camden Refugee Network
Annie Wheatley	Communications Department, Dorset County Council
PC Russ Woolley	Community Safety Section, West Dorset Police

Annex 2. Expert roundtable participants

Name	Organisation
Rushanara Ali	Home Office
Keith Best	Immigration Advisory Service
George Binette	Camden Borough Council
Andrew Brown	NASS
Phillip Colligan	Camden Borough Council
Heaven Crawley	AMRE Consulting
Jonathan Duke-Evans	Home Office
Richard Dunstan	Citizens Advice Bureau
Don Flynn	Joint Council for the Welfare of Immigrants
Tim Finch	Refugee Council
Edie Friedman	JCORE
Christoph Hauschild	German Federal Interior Ministry
Simon Hodgson	Scottish Refugee Council
Francesca Hopwood Road	ippr
Imran Hussain	Refugee Council
Helima Ismail	London Refugee Voice
Jonathon King	NASS
Sarah Kyambi	ippr
Nick Lane	ALM London
Miranda Lewis	ippr
Christopher Macdowell	ICAR
Forward Maisokwadzo	Presswise
Emily Miles	No 10 Policy Directorate
Alison Millar	NASS
Lisa Payne	National Children's Bureau
Elli Passmore	ippr
Nick Pearce	ippr
Heather Petch	Housing Association Charitable Trust
Andrew Puddephatt	Global Partners
Howard Reed	ippr
Will Somerville	Commission for Racial Equality
Sarah Spencer	COMPAS
Danny Sriskandarajah	ippr
Richard Stanton	Greater London Authority
Lisa Trickett	Birmingham City Council